YouTube

YouTube

YouTube

MAKING MONEY BY VIDEO SHARING

AND

ADVERTISING YOUR BUSINESS FOR FREE

By

Hui Ying

YouTube

© Copyright 2007 by Hui Ying. All rights reserved.

No part of this book may be reproduced, stored in a retrieval system, or transmitted by any means, electronic, mechanical, photocopying, recording, or otherwise, without written permission from the editor, author and author department.

ISBN: 978-0-9780460-6-4 (Paperback)

ISBN: 978-0-9780460-7-1 (e-book)

Library and Archives Canada Cataloguing in Publication

This book is printed on acid free paper.

This publication is designed to provide accurate and authoritative information that is up-to-date and current at the time of this publication. It is sold with the understanding that the publisher is not engaged in rendering any professional services, advise or recommendation.

Self-Help Publishers does not endorse any product or service or recommendation/advise in this publication. Any service or services provider listed in this publication assume full liability for their products and services and any claims direct or indirect arising from them.

Send your wholesale inquiries in U.S.A to Ingram Book Group, Baker & Taylor, and Nacscorp.

In United Kingdom and Europe send your wholesale inquiries to Bertram and Blackwell's.

For retail purchase visit your local Amazon and Barns and Nobles online bookstores or checkout with your local bookstore.

For reprint/co-publishing rights contact Self-Help Publishers at 3-445 Pioneer Dr. Kitchener ,ON, N2P 1L8 Canada or visit www.selfhelppublishers.com

Manufactured in United States of America and United Kingdom simultaneously

by arrangements with Self-Help publishers.

Cover design and layout by Lisa Walter

YouTube

ACKNOWLEDGEMENTS

About the YouTube
http://en.wikipedia.org/wiki/You-Tube

How You, Too, Can Use YouTube
By Pete Lerma

How To Make Money Embracing YouTube
http://pardonmyfrench.typepad.com/pardonmyfrench/2006/11/how_to_make_mon.html

It's Time to Learn About YouTube
By Daniel Henninger

What Can YouTube Learn From Search?
By Aaron Goldman

Forget free! Make money off your online video
© 2007 MSNBC Interactive

The YouTube Effect
By Moisés Naím - editor in chief of Foreign Policy.

YouTube Announces CBS Channel
By Pete Cashmore http://mashable.com/2006/10/09/youtube-announces-cbs-channel/

What Your Business Can Learn From YouTube
By Igor Mordkovich

YouTube

CONTENTS

What Is Youtube –Who We Are 1

Overview And Features 1

The Youtube Community 2

Traffic And Stats 3

Timeline 3

Demographics 3

Business Model 4

Content Partners 4

Youtube And Google 4

Frequently Asked Questions 6

What Is Youtube's Copyright Policy? 6

How Does Youtube Handle Inappropriate Content (I.E. Porn, Graphic/Violent Images, Etc)? 6

How Does Youtube Monetize Today? How Will You Monetize Youtube? Video Ads? Banner Ads? 6

What Does The Acquisition By Google Mean For The Community? 7

Will Youtube Now Have A Stronger International Presence? 7

How Video Sharing Works 8

User Generated Video Sharing 8

Video Sharing Scripts 10

Video Sharing Platform / White Label Providers 10

- Web Based Video Editing 10
- Wiki Based Video Indexing 11
- Bait Sites 11
- Youtube 12
- Our History 13
- Chad Hurley -Steve Chen- Jawed Karim .. 14
- Political Campaigning 16
- Media Recognition 16
- Press Coverage 18
- Revenue Model 18
- Recent Events 19
- Copyright Infringement 19
- Examples Of Infringement Complaints ... 21
- Use Of Acoustic Fingerprints 22
- 'Claim Your Content' Filtering System . 22
- Violence 22
- White House National Drug Control Involvement ... 23
- New York Times Reports Anti-US Attack Videos ... 23
- Banning 23
- Banning In Iran 23
- Banning In The US 23
- Banning In Australia 23
- Banning In Turkey 24

Banning In Thailand 24

Brazilian Model Lawsuit And Subsequent Banning 25

Domain Name Problem 25

Awards 26

Social Impact 26

Internet Celebrities 26

Band And Music Promotion 27

Influence On Other Sites 27

Fame Beyond Youtube 28

Technical Notes 29

Video Format 29

Content Accessibility 29

On Youtube 29

Outside Youtube 30

Downloading Videos 30

Viewing Deleted Videos 30

Index Sites 30

Most Popular Videos 31

The Youtube Effect 33

How A Technology For Teenagers Became A Force For Political And Economic Change. 33

Forget Free! Make Money Off Your Online Video 37

Some Sites Are Paying For Video In Order To Attract Budding Filmmakers 37

How You, Too, Can Use Youtube 39

Participatory Video Ads 39

Brand Channels 40

Grass-Root Approaches 40

What Can Youtube Learn From Search? 43

The Best Of The Search World 43

The Best Of The TV World 45

How To Make Money Embracing Youtube 47

Youtube Announces CBS Channel 49

AFTER ONE MONTH, CBS CONTENT AMONG MOST VIEWED VIDEOS ON YOUTUBE 51

What Your Business Can Learn From Youtube 57

Here Are Two Ways To Make Money Off 59

Youtube And GOOGLE Video 59

It's Time To Learn About Youtube 60

General Questions About You Tube 72

Signing Up 73

Solving Sign-Up And Log-In Issues 75

Enabling Cookies 75

Enable Cookies For Internet Explorer 7 75

Enable Cookies For Internet Explorer 6 76

Enable Cookies For Mozilla Firefox 2.X (PC) 77

Enable Cookies For Mozilla Firefox 1.X (PC) 77

Enable Cookies For Mozilla Firefox (Mac) 77

Enable Cookies For Safari 78

Clearing The Browser's Cache 78

Clear The Cache For Internet Explorer 7 78

Clear The Cache For Internet Explorer 6 79

Clear The Cache For Mozilla Firefox 2.X (PC).................................. 79

Clear The Cache For Mozilla Firefox 1.X (PC).................................. 79

Clear The Cache For Mozilla Firefox (Mac)...................................... 80

Clear The Cache For Safari 80

Watching Videos.. 82

Saving, Collecting, And Sharing Videos 85

From The Video Watch Page: 86

From Your Quicklist: 87

From Your Account:.. 87

Making, Uploading, And Promoting Videos 92

Uploading Videos To Youtube 97

File Size And Length Limits 100

Failed (Empty .Mov File) 106

Clearing Browser Cache 109

Internet Explorer 7... 109

Internet Explorer 6... 109

Mozilla Firefox 2 110

Mozilla Firefox 1.X 110

Safari 110

Clearing Browser Cookies 110

Internet Explorer 7 111

Internet Explorer 6 111

Mozilla Firefox 2.X 112

Mozilla Firefox 1.X 112

Safari 112

Record A Video 114

Choose A Video 114

Upload A Video 115

Videos 121

Chatting 121

Load Watched Videos Or Load Quicklist 122

Add Video By URL 123

To Close Your Account: 131

YouTube

YouTube

What is YouTube – Who we are

Overview and Features

Founded in February 2005, YouTube is the leader in online video, and the premier destination to watch and share original videos worldwide through a Web experience. YouTube allows people to easily upload and share video clips on www.YouTube.com and across the Internet through websites, mobile devices, blogs, and e-mail. YouTube has quickly become the leading destination on the Internet for video entertainment.

Everyone can watch videos on YouTube. People can see first-hand accounts of current events, find videos about their hobbies and interests, and discover the quirky and unusual. As more people capture special moments on video, YouTube is empowering them to become the broadcasters of tomorrow.

Some of the site's features include:

- Video embedding, which lets users insert a YouTube video into MySpace accounts, blogs, or other Web sites where anyone can watch them
- Public or private videos – users can elect to broadcast their videos publicly or share them privately with friends and family upon upload
- Subscriptions allow users to keep track of their favorite users' new videos
- Quick Capture – Users with a webcam and Flash software are able to instantly record video responses or normal videos onto the site rather than having to prerecord then upload the video
- TestTube – This is an area on the website where YouTube engineers and developers conduct alpha testing for new

features in development. Users are encouraged to participate in the development process and are welcome to evaluate the feature.

By registering, users are able to upload and share videos, save favorites, create playlists, and comment on the videos. YouTube is building a community that is highly motivated to watch and share videos. The YouTube service is free and will be supported by advertising.

The YouTube Community

YouTube is a place for people to engage in new ways with video by sharing, commenting on, and viewing videos. YouTube originally started as a personal video sharing service, and has quickly grown into the leading video entertainment destination on the Internet. Our users determine what is popular on the site, and can unleash their creativity and broadcast their talents to a global audience.

YouTube is creating a community for personal video, musicians, amateur filmmakers and comedians, and professional content owners. Our service is extremely viral, so if someone has a lot of talent and their content is really creative, users will be more likely to share the videos.

The explosion in consumer devices with video capability is giving users control over the videos they record, watch, and share, and YouTube is dedicated to making their experience as easy and entertaining as possible.

Unlike traditional broadcast channels, which have set windows for their programming, people can watch what they want, when they want on YouTube. We are focused on building the best user experience and the best platform for people to share their videos around the world. Anyone can broadcast themselves by creating content and distributing it through YouTube. And the community decides what is popular through their ratings and comments.

YouTube is an open community and encourages users to send in their thoughts and comments about their experiences on the site. YouTube understands that each and every user makes the site what it is and welcomes them to get involved to help create new features and be a part of new developments on the site.

YouTube also is actively exploring a variety of ways to help the community to monetize content, and expect to announce something in the coming months that users will embrace. At the end of the day, it's all about the community and we will continue to do what we can to make the user experience a prosperous one.

Traffic and Stats

As you can imagine, interest in the site continues to increase at a dramatic rate. While we're more focused on providing our community with the features that they are asking for and giving them the best possible user experience than we are in crunching numbers, we continue to be the leader online video.

Timeline

YouTube was founded in February 2005 from a garage in Menlo Park, and development began immediately. We started a public preview in May of 2005 and officially launched the company and service later that year in December. In November of 2006, YouTube was acquired by Google and continues to operate as an independent subsidiary.

Demographics

Our user base is 18-55, spanning all geographies. With such a large and diverse user base, YouTube offers something for everyone.

Business Model

YouTube is pursuing advertising as its business model, and is exploring a range of possibilities including PVAs (participatory video ads) promotions, sponsorships, contextual-based advertising, traditional banner advertising, etc. But more than anything else, we're committed to providing the best consumer experience to watch, upload, and share videos. When building a community, it is critical to get the model right.

Content Partners

YouTube is a stage for everyone, including traditional media companies, filmmakers, record labels, movie studios, comedians and more. With the shift happening in digital media entertainment and a new clip culture evolving, professional content creators are recognizing the potential of promoting themselves and their programming on YouTube to reach a vast, new audience. As such, YouTube has evolved into a powerful monetization and promotional platform.

One type of partnership is no more important than any other, just as one type of content is no more important than any other. User generated and "amateur" content carries as much importance as professionally created videos. We are focused on providing the greatest depth and breadth possible for our users, and the thousands of partnerships we have with content creators and media companies, both big and small, are a testament to that.

YouTube and Google

YouTube is an independent subsidiary of Google, Inc., having been acquired by the leader in search and online advertising services in November of 2006.

YouTube

Google and YouTube share the vision of enabling anyone to find, upload, watch and share original videos worldwide, and the dedication to innovate with video to offer compelling services for our users and for content owners.

The exciting and powerful platform YouTube has built complements Google's mission to organize the world's information and make it universally accessible and useful.

By working together, YouTube and Google will be able to offer a better, more comprehensive experience for our users and new opportunities for content owners and advertisers. From individuals with video cell phones to major studios with professional content, we're excited to create the world's next generation video platform together.

Frequently Asked Questions

What is YouTube's copyright policy?

We don't control the content on our site. Our users post the content on YouTube—including videos, comments, and ratings. Our community guidelines and clear messaging on the site make it clear that users must own or have permission from copyright holders to post any videos.

We take copyright issues very seriously. We prohibit users from uploading infringing material and we cooperate with copyright holders to identify and promptly remove infringing content.

How does YouTube handle inappropriate content (i.e. porn, graphic/violent images, etc)?

Our policy prohibits inappropriate content on YouTube. Our community understands the rules and effectively polices the site for inappropriate material. The users can flag content that they feel is inappropriate and once it is flagged, YouTube reviews the content and removes it from the system within minutes if it violates our Terms of Use. This combined with our proprietary technology helps us to enforce the rules. We also disable the accounts of repeat offenders.

How does YouTube monetize today? How will you monetize YouTube? Video ads? Banner ads?

Today, YouTube serves untargeted ads on some of its pages. We're committed to preserving the quality of the user experience and we are also interested in exploring how we can further benefit content owners through different ways of sponsorship. We have conducted a variety of tests to determine what monetization strategies are best for content providers and best for users, and we will integrating the results of those tests into our future efforts.

What does the acquisition by Google mean for the community?

YouTube's business was built, in large part, by our community. The user experience will not change—we are committed to this and will continue to listen to our community's feedback. The community is still in control on YouTube, and, at the end of the day, they decide what's entertaining.

Our independence empowers us to continue to build the best, most entertaining video experience on the Internet. Google's resources and technology leadership will provide us with the flexibility to expand and improve that experience further.

Will YouTube now have a stronger international presence?

YouTube continues to operate independently, completely within the United States. However, we are committed to "internationalizing" YouTube by translating services and features into each country's native language.

What are the criteria you use to establish what will be a featured video? Is it purely driven by the most-viewed/rated/discussed/etc, or are there other factors?

Videos that appear in the "Featured Videos" section on the home page are chosen through a variety of sources. While users can send videos the YouTube editorial team for consideration, they also can rate and share videos to help make them popular on the site. Our editorial team reviews the videos users have made popular and features the most entertaining and compelling content on the home page.

How Video Sharing Works

Video sharing refers to websites or software where a user can distribute their video clips. Some services may charge, but the bulk of them offer free services. Many services have options for **private sharing** and other publication options. **Video sharing** services can be classified into several categories, among them: user generated **video sharing websites**, **video sharing platform / white label** providers and **web based video editing**. Please note that websites that are solely search engines and do not provide the hosting of their video content (such as SingingFish) are not included in this article.

User generated video sharing

User generated sites mostly offer free services whereby users can **upload video clips** and share it with the masses. Many sites place restrictions on the file size, duration, subject matter and format of the uploaded video file. Most sites don't allow nudity, though each site makes judgement calls on what qualifies inappropriate content. Some sites also flag adult material to keep it out of their public pool of content. Some sites screen all their content before it is published and others approve first and use community features to filter out inappropriate content "after-the-fact." Also a lot of user video is placed on the site, as well as people's stories.

Web sites in this category include (in alphabetical order):

- Angry Alien
- Blennus.com
- Break.com
- BroadcaZt
- Bubblare.se
- Dachix
- Dailymotion

YouTube

- EngageMedia
- FlixHunt
- Google Video
- Grouper
- GUBA
- iFilm
- LabAction, Biology Video Sharing.
- LiveDigital
- OneWorldTV
- Metacafe
- MSN Soapbox
- Myspace
- Online Talent Network
- Revver
- Sharkle
- Stage6-Divx
- SUMO.tv (Also operates its own TV channel, SKY channel 146 in the UK)
- TheVideoSense
- ToKillFor.com
- Twango
- uVu
- viewurself.com
- Vimeo
- vMix
- XTube
- YouTube
- ZippyVideos
- Zooppa.com (an online advertising generator based on crowdsourcing)

There are also sites that are intended more for private sharing of videos. Among sites in this category are:

- Phanfare

Video Sharing Scripts

Youtube's success sparked the development of various video sharing scripts, which made it possible for people with little knowledge or skills to create video sharing communities.

Scripts in this category include (in alphabetical order):

- ClipShare

Video Sharing Platform / White Label Providers

Platform and White Label Providers sell the technology to various parties that allow them to create the services of the aforementioned **"User Generated Video Sharing"** websites with the client's brand. Just as Akamai and other companies host and manage video/image/audio for many companies, these white-labels **host video content**. Many of these companies also offer their own user generated **video sharing website** both for commercial purposes and to show off their platform Websites in this category include (in alphabetical order):

- Homemovie.com
- VideoEgg
- vMix

Web based video editing

Web based video editing sites generally offer the **"user generated video sharing"** website in addition to some form of editing application. Some of these applications simply allow the user to crop a video into a smaller clip. Other services have invested much time and effort into replicating the same functionality that has previously only been available via Windows Movie Maker, iMovie and other client-side applications that run outside of a web page. Some of these applications are based in AJAX and others in Flash.

Some websites also offer downloadable editors but they will not be listed here due to the number of pre-existing video editors.

Websites in this category include (in alphabetical order):

- Clesh (the consumer version of FORscene)
- Homemovie.com
- JumpCut
- Motionbox
- Movie Masher
- StashSpace

Wiki based video indexing

A few wiki websites have begun to sort and index the videos posted on popular video sharing sites. This includes:

- IndexTube - IndexTube webpage
- SaneScreen - SaneScreen webpage
- Vidspedia - Vidspedia webpage

The videos are not hosted on these sites, but they are embedded.

Bait Sites

Movie6.net is a common MPAA bait site in which an IP Tracker is used to find the IPs of those who pirate movies.

YouTube

YouTube is the most popular video sharing website where users can upload, view, and share video clips. Videos can be rated, and the average rating and the number of times a video has been watched are both published.

Founded in February 2005 by three former employees of PayPal, the San Bruno-based service utilizes Adobe Flash technology to display video. The wide variety of site content includes movie and TV clips and music videos, as well as amateur content such as videoblogging and short original videos. Currently staffed by 67 employees,[1] the company was named *TIME* magazine's "Invention of the Year" for 2006.[2] In October 2006, Google Inc. announced that it had reached a deal to acquire the company for US$1.65 billion in Google's stock. The deal closed on 13 November 2006.[3]

The site is praised as one the most user friendly sites on the Internet. Unregistered users can watch most videos on the site while registered users have the ability to upload an unlimited number of videos. Related videos, determined by the title and tags, appear to the right of the video. In the second year, the site gave users the ability to post responses and subscribe to any registered user.

YouTube History

YouTube's early headquarters in San Mateo

YouTube was founded by Chad Hurley, Steve Chen, and Jawed Karim, who were all early employees of PayPal.[4] Prior to PayPal, Hurley studied design at Indiana University of Pennsylvania. Chen and Karim studied computer science together at the University of Illinois at Urbana-Champaign.[5] The domain name "YouTube.com" was activated on February 15, 2005,[6] and the website was developed over the following months. The creators offered the public a preview of the site in May 2005, and six months later, YouTube made its official debut.

YouTube

Chad Hurley -Steve Chen- Jawed Karim

YouTube's current headquarters in San Bruno

Like many technology start-ups, YouTube was started as an angel-funded enterprise in a small and inexpensive office or garage. In November of 2005, venture capital firm Sequoia Capital invested an initial $3.5 million;[7] additionally, Roelof Botha, partner of the firm and former CFO of PayPal, joined the YouTube board of directors. In April 2006, Sequoia put an additional $8 million into the company, which had experienced a boom of popularity and growth in just its first few months.[8]

During the summer of 2006, YouTube was one of the fastest-growing websites on the World Wide Web,[9] and was ranked as the 5th most popular website on Alexa, far outpacing even MySpace's growth.[10] According to a July 16, 2006 survey, 100 million clips are viewed daily on YouTube, with an additional 65,000 new videos uploaded per 24 hours. The site has almost 20 million visitors each month, according to Nielsen/NetRatings,[11] where around 44% are female, 56% male, and the 12- to 17-year-old age group is dominant.[12] YouTube's pre-eminence in the online video market is staggering. According to the website Hitwise.com, YouTube commands up to 64% of the UK online video market.[13]

Wikinews has news related to:

Google purchases YouTube for $1.65 billion

On October 9, 2006, it was announced that the company would be purchased by Google for US$1.65 billion in stock. The purchase agreement between Google and YouTube came after YouTube presented three agreements with media companies in an attempt to escape the threat of copyright-infringement lawsuits. YouTube will continue to operate independently, and the company's 67 employees and its co-founders will continue working within the company.[14] The deal to acquire YouTube closed on November 13. It is Google's biggest purchase of that time.[15]

Political campaigning

Political candidates for the 2008 US Presidential election have been using YouTube as an outlet for advertising their candidacy. Voters can easily look up propaganda and make videos supporting or demoting presidential candidates of their own, specifically those for Barack Obama and Hillary Clinton. The US media has often commented that YouTube played a significant role in the 2006 defeat of Republican Senator George Allen due to a video clip of him making allegedly racist remarks that was replayed continuously by YouTube viewers during his campaign. Recently, French and Italian politicians, such as Antonio Di Pietro, have also been using the site as part of their campaigns.

Media recognition

In its short time on the web, YouTube has grown quickly and received much attention. Online word-of-mouth has been primarily responsible for YouTube's growth since its inception, and gave the site its first surge of publicity when it hosted the popular *Saturday Night Live* short *Lazy Sunday*.[16] However, YouTube's official policy prohibits submission of copyrighted material, and NBC Universal, owners of *SNL*, soon decided to take action.

In February 2006, NBC asked for the removal of some of its copyrighted content from YouTube, including *Lazy Sunday* and 2006 Olympics clips.[7][17] The following month, in an attempt to strengthen its policy against copyright infringement, YouTube set a 10-minute maximum limit on video length (except for content submitted via its Director Program, which specifically hosts original material by amateur filmmakers). However, the real cutoff is 10:58.[citation needed] This restriction is often circumvented by uploaders, who instead split their original video into smaller segments, each shorter than the 10-minute limit.

Though YouTube had done its part to comply with NBC's demands, the incident made the news, giving YouTube its most prominent publicity yet. As the site continued to grow, NBC began to realize the possibilities, and in June 2006 made an unusual move. The network had reconsidered its actions and was announcing a strategic partnership with YouTube. Under the terms of the partnership, an official NBC channel was set up on YouTube, showcasing promotional clips for the series *The Office*. YouTube will also promote NBC's videos throughout its site.[18]

CBS, which had previously also asked YouTube to remove several of its clips, followed suit in July 2006. In a statement indicative of how the traditional media industry's perception of YouTube (and similar sites) has changed, Sean McManus, president of CBS News and Sports noted:

> Our inclination now is, the more exposure we get from clips like that, the better it is for CBS News and the CBS television network, so in retrospect we probably should have embraced the exposure, and embraced the attention it was bringing CBS, instead of being parochial and saying 'let's pull it down.'[19]

In August of 2006, YouTube announced that, within 18 months, it hopes to offer every music video ever created, while still remaining free of charge. Warner Music Group and EMI have confirmed that they are among the companies in talks to implement this plan.[20] In September Warner Music and YouTube signed a deal, in which YouTube will be allowed to host every music video Warner produced while sharing a portion of the advertisement income. Additionally, user-created videos on YouTube will be allowed to use Warner songs in their soundtracks.[21]

On October 9, CBS, along with Universal Music Group and Sony BMG Music Entertainment, also agreed to provide content to YouTube.[22]

On January 29, 2007, the co-founder of YouTube, Chad Hurley, announced that the on-line video service will pay its active users, who should also be true copyright owners, a part of the website's revenue gained from advertising. However, at the World Economic Forum, Mr. Hurley did not mention a concrete amount of money that YouTube will pay its contributors.[23]

Press coverage

Time Magazine featured a YouTube screen with a foil mirror as its annual Person of the Year citing user created media such as YouTube, and featuring its creators and several content creators. The *Wall Street Journal* and *New York Times* have also reviewed content posted on YouTube, and its effects on recruiting and corporate communications in 2006. PC World Magazine has also named YouTube as the 9th of the Top 10 Best Products of 2006.[24] Because of its acquisition by Google, it is sometimes referred to as "GooTube."[25]

Revenue model

Before being bought by Google, YouTube stated that its business model is advertising-based. Some industry commentators have speculated that YouTube's running costs — specifically the bandwidth required — may be as high as US$1 million per-month,[26] thereby fueling criticisms that the company, like many Internet start-ups, did not have a viably implemented business model. Advertisements were launched on the site beginning in March 2006. In April, YouTube started using Google AdSense. YouTube subsequently stopped using AdSense. Given its traffic levels, video streams and pageviews, some have calculated that YouTube's potential revenues could be in the millions per month[27].

Recent events

Copyright infringement

YouTube policy does not allow content to be uploaded by anyone not permitted by United States copyright law to do so, and the company frequently removes uploaded infringing content. Nonetheless, a large amount of it continues to be uploaded. Generally, unless the copyright holder reports them, YouTube only discovers these videos via indications within the YouTube community through self-policing. The primary way in which YouTube identifies the content of a video is through the search terms that uploaders associate with clips. Some users have taken to creating alternative words as search terms to be entered when uploading specific type of files (similar to the deliberate misspelling of band names on MP3 filesharing networks). For a short time, members could also report one another. The service offers a flagging feature, intended as a means for reporting questionable content, including that which might constitute copyright infringement. However, the feature can be susceptible to abuse; for a time, some users were flagging other users' original content for copyright violations, purely out of spite. YouTube proceeded to remove copyright infringement from the list of offenses flaggable by members.

Hollywood remains divided on YouTube, as "'[t]he marketing guys love YouTube and the legal guys hate it.'"[28] Further,

> While lawyers are demanding filtering technology, many Hollywood execs actually enjoy the fact that YouTube only takes down clips when they request it. "If I found part of a successful show up on YouTube today, I'd probably pull it down immediately . . . If I had a show that wasn't doing so well in the ratings and could use the promotion, I wouldn't be in a rush to do that."[28]

Content owners are not just targeting YouTube for copyright infringements on the site, but they are also targeting third party websites that link to infringing content on YouTube and other video sharing sites. For example QuickSilverScreen vs. Fox[29] Daily Episodes vs. Fox[30] and Columbia vs. Slashfilm.[31] The liability of linking remains a grey area with cases for and against. The law in the US currently leans towards website owners being liable for infringing links[32] although they are often protected by the DMCA providing they take down infringing content when issued with a takedown notice. However, a recent court ruling in the US found Google not to be liable for linking to infringing content (Perfect 10 v. Google, Inc.).

Examples of infringement complaints

On October 5, 2006 the Japanese Society for Rights of Authors, Composers and Publishers (JASRAC) had their copyright complaints regarding Japanese media on YouTube finalized. Thousands of media from popular Japanese artists (such as Tokyo Jihen and various other music including Jpop) were removed.

When CBS and Universal Music Group signed agreements to provide content to YouTube they announced that they would use new technology that will help them find copyrighted material and remove it.[22]

TV journalist Robert Tur filed the first lawsuit against the company in Summer 2006, alleging copyright infringement for hosting a number of famous news clips without permission. The case has yet to be resolved.[33][34]

On November 9, 2006 Artie Lange said his lawyer were in talks with YouTube, after finding his entire DVD, *It's the Whiskey Talking*, available for free on their site. Artie said he will either demand money from them, or else he will sue.[35]

Viacom and the British Broadcasting Corporation both demanded YouTube to take down more than 200,000 videos.[36]

Wikinews has news related to:

Viacom sues YouTube, owner Google, for more than 1 billion dollars

Viacom announced it was suing YouTube, and its owner Google, for more than $1 billion in the United States District Court for the Southern District of New York. Viacom claims that YouTube has over 160,000 of their videos on their website without their permission.[37][38]

Use of acoustic fingerprints

On October 12, 2006, YouTube announced that because of recent agreements with high-profile content creators, they were now required to use anti-piracy software. The software uses an audio-signature technology that can spot a low-quality copy of a licensed music video or other content. YouTube would have to substitute an approved version of the clip or take the material down automatically. Analysts noted removal of content based on such a system might negatively impact user satisfaction. This is frustrating for viewers who upload anime music videos, because most AMVs use licensed music content; however, often said music is acquired illegally as well.[39]

'Claim Your Content' Filtering System

On April 16, 2007, Google's CEO Eric Schmitt presented a keynote speech at the NAB Convention in Las Vegas. During the Q&A, Schmidt announced that YouTube was close to enacting a content filtering system to remove infringing content from the service. The new system, called "Claim Your Content," will automatically identify copyrighted material so that it can be removed. [40]

Violence

Main article: Cyber-bullying#Influence

On June 1, 2006, the evening ITV News bulletin reported that YouTube and sites like it were encouraging violence and bullying amongst teenagers, who were filming fights on their mobile phones (*see happy slapping*), and then uploading them to YouTube. While the site provides a function for reporting excessively violent videos, the news report stated that communication with the company was difficult.[41]

White House National Drug Control involvement

In September 2006, the Office of National Drug Control Policy (ONDCP) began running anti-drug messages through the YouTube System.[42] In response, many YouTube users began uploading rebuttals and rating the public service announcements down. Since mid-September, the ONDCP has removed the ability to rate or comment on any of their messages as a result.

New York Times reports anti-US attack videos

On October 5, 2006, *The New York Times* reported on the proliferation of what they considered to be anti-U.S. Iraqi insurgent attack videos on YouTube.[43]

Banning

Banning in Iran

On December 3, 2006, Iran blocked YouTube and several other sites in an attempt to impede "corrupting" foreign films and music.[44]

Banning in the US

On February 16, 2007 the Chronicle of Higher Education reported that Brigham Young University has blocked campus access to YouTube to prevent students from viewing violence and pornography.[45]

Banning in Australia

Australian NSW schools have blocked the site due to the New South Wales Department of Education and Training filtering system which most schools proxy through.

Banning in Turkey

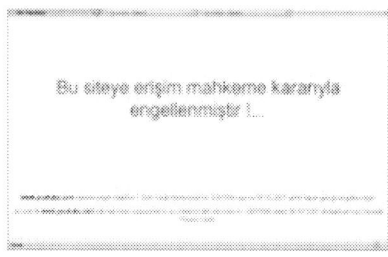

YouTube was blocked in Turkey. "Access to this site is blocked by court order".

Turkey blocked YouTube on March 6, 2007 for letting videos insulting Turks and Atatürk, the founder of modern Turkey, to be shown, in an escalation of what some call a "virtual war" between Greeks and Turks on YouTube, with people from each side posting videos to belittle and berate the other.[46] The video that caused banning alleged Turks and Atatürk to be homosexuals. The video was first mentioned on Turkish CNN and the Istanbul public prosecutor sued YouTube for insulting Turkishness.[47] The court suspended access to YouTube pending removal of the video. The ban was strongly criticized as censorship in the press and by the general public. YouTube lawyers sent documentary of removal to public prosecutor and access was restored on March 9, 2007.[48]

Banning in Thailand

During the week of March 8th, YouTube was blocked in Thailand.[49] Many bloggers believed the reason YouTube was blocked was because of a video of the former Prime Minister Thaksin Shinawatra's speech on CNN. However, the government did not confirm or give reasons for the ban. YouTube was accessible from March 10th.

On the night of April 3rd, YouTube was again blocked in Thailand.[50] The government cited a video on the site that it called "insulting" to King Bhumibol Adulyadej.[51]. However, the Ministry of Information and Communication Technology claimed that it would unblock YouTube in a few days, after websites containing references to this video are blocked instead of the entire website.[52] Communications Minister Sitthichai Pookaiyaudom said, "When they decide to withdraw the clip, we will withdraw the ban."[53] Shortly after this incident the internet technology blog Mashable was banned from Thailand over the reporting of the YouTube clips in question. [54]

Brazilian model lawsuit and subsequent banning

YouTube is being sued by Brazilian model and MTV VJ Daniela Cicarelli (better known as Ronaldo's ex-fiancée) on the grounds that the site is making available a video footage made by a paparazzo, in which she and her boyfriend are having sex on a Spanish beach. The lawsuit requires that YouTube be blocked in Brazil until all copies of the video are removed. On Saturday, January 6, 2007, a legal injunction ordered that filters be put in place to prevent users in Brazil from accessing the website.[55][56]

The effectiveness of the measure has been questioned, since the video is not available only on YouTube, but rather has become an Internet phenomenon. On Tuesday, January 9, 2007, a higher court overturned the original decision, ordering the filters removed, although the footage itself remained forbidden, but without technical support for its blockage.[57] After the banning of YouTube in Brazil there has been a website called brtube.com as an unofficial replacement for YouYube in Brazil.

Domain name problem

YouTube's immense success has unintentionally affected the business for an American company, Universal Tube and Rollerform

Equipment Corp., whose website, http://www.utube.com, has frequently been shut down by extremely high numbers of visitors unsure about the spelling of YouTube's domain name.[58] At the beginning of November 2006, Universal Tube filed suit in federal court against YouTube.[59]

Utube, based out of Perrysburg, Ohio, has requested as part of their suit that the youtube.com domain be transferred to them.[60]

Awards

YouTube has recently announced its first YouTube Video Awards for the year 2006. Categories include "'most adorable' video ever" and "most creative." Nominees include Peter Oakley (geriatric1927), LonelyGirl15, thewinekone, Renetto and Chad Vader. [61][62]

2006 Awards[63]:

- Most Creative - *Here It Goes Again* OK Go
- Best Comedy - *Smosh Short 2: Stranded* Smosh
- Best Commentary - *Hotness Prevails* thewinekone
- Best Series - *Ask A Ninja* digtalfilmmaker
- Best Music Video - *Say It Possible* Terra Naomi
- Most Inspirational - *Free Hugs Campaign* PeaceOnEarth123
- Most Adorable - *Kiwi* Madyeti47

Social impact

Internet celebrities

YouTube's popularity has led to the creation of many YouTube Internet celebrities, popular individuals who have attracted significant publicity in their home countries from their videos.[64] The most subscribed YouTube member, as of April 6, 2007, is lonelygirl15.[65] For these users, the Internet fame has had various unexpected effects. By way of example, YouTube user and former receptionist Brooke Brodack from Massachusetts has been signed by NBC's Carson Daly for an 18-month development contract.[66] Another has been the uncovered fictional blog of lonelygirl15, now discovered to be the work of New Zealand actress Jessica Rose and some film directors. In 2007, a Dutch vocalist and songwriter named Esmée Denters was signed to a recording contract by Billy Mann based on her YouTube appearances.[67][68]

Band and music promotion

YouTube has also become a means of promoting bands and their music. One such example is OK Go which got a huge radio hit and an MTV Video Music Awards performance out of the treadmill video for Here It Goes Again.[69][70] In the same light, a video broadcasting the Free Hugs Campaign with accompanying music by the Sick Puppies led to instant fame for both the band and the campaign, with more campaigns taking place in different parts of the world. The main character of the video, Juan Mann has also achieved fame, being interviewed on Australian news programs, even appearing on The Oprah Winfrey Show.[71]

Influence on other sites

Many other sites have used the -tube ending, including PornoTube and LesbianTube.

Fame beyond YouTube

A number of figures have grown to prominence and become Internet phenomena on the basis of their appearance in YouTube videos. These include:

- Andy McKee
- Barats and Bereta
- Abbeynainsley
- boh3m3
- BowieChick
- Brooke Brodack (Brookers)
- Chad Vader
- Chan Yuet Tung, a.k.a. the Bus Uncle
- Emmalina
- Erik Mongrain
- Esmée Denters
- GiR2007
- Jeong-Hyun Lim, a.k.a. Funtwo
- Juan Mann
- Liam Kyle Sullivan, a.k.a. Kelly (The *Shoes* Song)
- Lisa Donovan, a.k.a LisaNova
- lonelygirl15
- Luke Johnson
- Mr. Safety, a.k.a SMPFilms
- Naztradamix, a.k.a. Randy Hayes
- Noah Kalina
- Olde English
- Peter Oakley, a.k.a geriatric1927
- Renetto
- Riven Phoenix
- Smosh
- Stevie Ryan
- Terra Naomi
- TheHill88
- thewinekone

Brooke Brodack is considered the first person to move from Youtube to mainstream media, when she signed an 18-month development deal with Carson Daly's production company.[72] In January, 2007, it was announced that Lisa Donovan, a.k.a. LisaNova, was going to appear as a cast member during the 12th season of Fox's sketch comedy show *MADtv*.[73]

Technical notes

Video format

YouTube's video playback technology is based on Macromedia's FlashPlayer 7 and uses the Sorenson Spark H.263 video codec. This technology allows YouTube to display videos with quality comparable to more established video playback technologies (such as Windows Media Player, Realplayer or Apple's Quicktime Player) that generally require the user to download and install a web browser plugin in order to watch video. Flash itself requires a plug-in, but the Flash 7 plug-in is generally considered to be present on approximately 90% of Internet-connected computers.[74] Alternatively, users can use a number of websites to download the videos to their own computers.

YouTube converts videos into .FLV (Adobe Flash Video) format after uploading.[75] The extension is then stripped from the file (Extension can be found again with TrID). The different files are stored in obscurely named subdomains, to make ripping the videos difficult.

YouTube officially accepts uploaded videos in WMV, AVI, MOV and MPEG formats.[76]

Content accessibility

On YouTube

Users may submit videos in several common-file formats (such as .mpeg and .avi). YouTube automatically converts them to the H.263 variant of Flash Video (with extension .flv) and makes them available for online viewing. Flash Video is a popular video format among large hosting sites due to its wide compatibility.

Outside YouTube

Each video is accompanied by the full HTML markup for linking to it and/or embedding it within another page; a small addition to the markup for the latter will make the video autoplay when the page is accessed. These simple cut-and-paste options are popular particularly with users of social/networking sites. Poor experiences have, however, been cited by members of such sites,[77] where autoplaying embedded YouTube videos has been reported to slow down page loading time or even to cause browsers to crash.

Downloading videos

YouTube itself does not make it easy to download and save videos for offline viewing or editing, but several third-party web sites (e.g. SaveTube) applications, browser extensions (e.g. the UnPlug or VideoDownloader Firefox extensions or FLVR and Free YouTube Converter) and web sites exist for that purpose. Alternatively, most .flv files can be copied from Temporary Internet Files (in Windows) to a permanent folder. The .flv files can then be converted to more popular formats using various tools. [2]

Viewing deleted videos

YouTube videos which are flagged as deleted are not necessarily deleted physically. It is possible to recover and download these videos by using web applications such as the Deleted YouTube Video Viewer.

Index sites

Websites are available that offer an index service and arrange the content on YouTube by relativity, i.e. links arranged by order of seasons and episodes of a certain show. Examples include TVLinks, NetworkOne Australia, and WikiRemote.

Most Popular Videos

The most viewed videos on YouTube (10 million views or more) as of April 6, 2007.

46.06 million – *Evolution of Dance* – Judson Laipply
22.0 million – *Pokémon Theme Music Video* – Ian Hecox and Anthony Padilla

19.9 million – *Famous Last Words* – My Chemical Romance
19.5 million – *SNL Digital Short - A Special Christmas Gift (Uncensored)* – Saturday Night Live
17.8 million – *Guitar* – Jeong-Hyun Lim
16.6 million – *Quick Change Artists on America's Got Talent* – America's Got Talent

15.7 million – *Shoes* – Liam Kyle Sullivan
14.4 million – *OK Go - Here It Goes Again* – OK Go
13.9 million – *Hey clip* – Tasha and Dishka
12.9 million – *Free Hugs Campaign* – Juan Mann
12.8 million – *Real Life Simpsons Intro* – The Simpsons
12.6 million – *Hahaha* – BlackOleg
12.4 million – *Urban Ninja* – Trickster Xin of EMC California
11.9 million – *Ronaldinho: A Touch of Gold* – Nike
10.3 million – *lion sleep tonight* – Pat & Stanley

YouTube

YouTube

The YouTube Effect

How a technology for teenagers became a force for political and economic change.

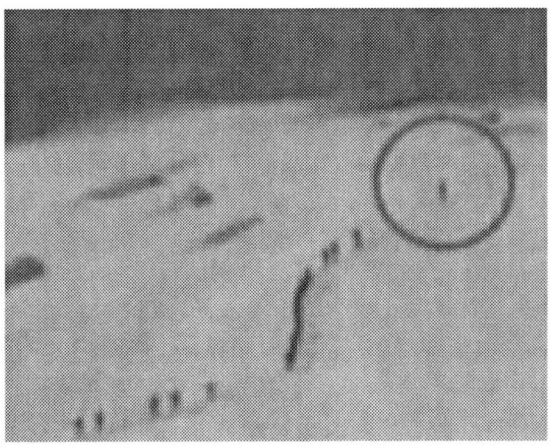

Red-handed: Chinese soldiers shot down Tibetan monks, women, and children in cold blood, but a climber caught them on tape. See more "YouTube effect" videos here.

A video shows a single line of people slowly trudging up a snow-covered footpath. A shot is heard; the first person in line falls. A voice-over says, "They are shooting them like dogs." Another shot, and another body drops to the ground. A uniformed Chinese soldier fires his rifle again. Then, a group of soldiers examines the fallen bodies.

These images were captured high in the Himalayas by a member of a mountaineering expedition who claims to have stumbled upon the killing. The video first aired on Romanian television, but it only gained worldwide attention when it was posted on YouTube, the popular video-sharing Web site. Human rights groups explained that the slain were a group of Tibetan refugees that included monks, women, and children. According to the Chinese government, the soldiers had fired in self-defense after they were attacked by 70 refugees. The posted video seems to render that explanation absurd. The U.S. ambassador to China quickly lodged a complaint protesting China's treatment of the refugees.

Welcome to the YouTube effect. It is the phenomenon whereby video clips, often produced by individuals acting on their own, are rapidly disseminated throughout the world thanks to video-sharing Web sites such as YouTube, Google Video, and others. Every month, YouTube receives 20 million visitors, who watch 100 million video clips a day. There are 65,000 new videos posted every day. Most of the videos are frivolous, produced by and for teenagers. But some are serious. YouTube includes videos posted by terrorists, human rights groups, and U.S. soldiers in Iraq. Some are clips of incidents that have political consequences or document important trends, such as global warming, illegal immigration, and corruption. Some videos reveal truths. Others spread disinformation, propaganda, and outright lies. All are part of the YouTube effect.

Fifteen years ago, the world marveled at the fabled "CNN effect." The expectation was that the unblinking eyes of TV cameras, beyond the reach of censors, would bring greater accountability and transparency to governments and the international system. These expectations were, in some sense, fulfilled. Since the early 1990s, electoral frauds that might have remained hidden were exposed, democratic uprisings energized, famines contained, and wars started or stopped, thanks to the CNN effect. But the YouTube effect will be even more intense. Although the BBC, CNN, and other international news operations employ thousands of professional journalists, they will never be as omnipresent as millions of people carrying a cell phone that can record video. Thanks to their ubiquity, the world was able to witness a shooting on a 19,000-foot mountain pass.

This phenomenon is amplified by a double echo chamber: One is produced when content first posted on the Web is re-aired by mainstream TV networks. The second occurs when television moments, even the most fleeting, gain a permanent presence thanks to bloggers or activists who redistribute them through Web sites like YouTube. Activists everywhere are recognizing the power of citizen-produced and Web-distributed videos as the ultimate testimony. The human rights group Witness arms individuals in conflict zones with video cameras so they can record and expose human rights abuses. Electoral watchdogs are taping elections. Even Islamic terrorists have adapted to this trend. Al Qaeda created a special media production unit called Al Sahab ("The Cloud"), which routinely posts its videos online, with the realistic expectation that they will be picked up by major media outlets and other Web sites.

The YouTube effect has brought other mixed blessings. It is now harder to know what to believe. How do we know that what we see in a video clip posted by a "citizen journalist" is not a montage? How do we know, for example, that the YouTube video of terrorized American soldiers crying and praying for their lives while under fire was filmed in Iraq and not staged somewhere else to manipulate public opinion? The more than 86,000 people who viewed it in the first 10 days of its posting will never know.

Governments are already feeling the heat of the YouTube effect. The U.S. military recently ordered its soldiers to stop posting videos unless they have been vetted. The Iranian government restricts connection speeds to limit its people's access to video streaming. These measures have not stopped the proliferation of Web videos shot by U.S. soldiers in Iraq, or savvy Iranians from viewing the images they want to see. And, though Beijing has been effective in censoring the content its citizens can view, it has yet to figure out a way to prevent a growing number of videos of peasant rebellions from being posted online. In the long run, all such efforts will fail.

When it comes to having faith in what we see online, the good news is that the YouTube effect is already creating a strong demand for reliable guides—individuals, institutions, and technologies that we can trust to help us sort facts from lies. That is important, because the hope of countering the downsides of the YouTube effect will never come from government intervention. Markets and democracy do a much better job of filtering the bad from the good in the confusing tsunami of Web videos coming our way. The millions of bloggers who are constantly watching, fact-checking, and exposing mistakes are a powerful example of "the wisdom of crowds" at work. Sure, markets and democracies often fail or disappoint. But the openness these political and economic forces promote are now being assisted by a technology that is as omnipresent as we are.

Forget free! Make money off your online video

Some sites are paying for video in order to attract budding filmmakers

YouTube is currently the go-to site for viral video, but some Web sites are now offering financial incentives to burgeoning filmmakers in hopes of getting higher quality video and more online traffic. "Most" senior producer Tony Maciulis reports

With nearly 100 million videos viewed each day, it's hard to beat the audience that YouTube has built.

But YouTube, for all its size and splendor, also has vulnerabilities. A new generation of viral video sites is trying to beat the powerhouse at its own game by answering the two major criticisms -- a need for revenue and greater quality control of the clips.

It is definitely a household name -- the Kleenex of video sites -- but YouTube can be enormously tedious. There are simply too many videos, and while you occasionally find that "Diet Coke and Mentos" gem, most of them are pretty lame.

But now a couple of sites are offering some incentive to separate the wheat from the chaff.

The video site Break.com is offering $400 for videos, and up to $2,000 for animated films. The goal is to attract quality films from budding filmmakers and not just the cell phone camera cat antics you frequently see at YouTube. The typical length is about 10 minutes, so these are really more like film shorts.

So far Break.com has paid out about $300,000 for videos, in the hopes that the better quality control will bring in ad dollars that YouTube may not be able to attract.

Another site getting some buzz is Revver.com. This site sticks ads onto user video clips, and then pays the user a share of the profits. The more clicks a video receives, the more money a user can make.

Revver just signed a major deal with Verizon to deliver video clips to cell phones. The service will cost subscribers $15 per month. Of course, if you can wait until you're in front of your computer, the videos are free.

The whole business of video sharing is still in its infancy, and it is difficult to hazard a guess about which of the business models will ultimately succeed. One thing seems certain -- $1.65 billion for a site with no current revenue stream is a real gamble.

How You, Too, Can Use YouTube

So you think you might... possibly... want to consider... maybe... placing your brand on YouTube? Why not? After all, it's one of the most popular sites online. In fact, in July, YouTube had over 16 million unique visitors.

Recently, Lee Gomes from "The Wall Street Journal" estimated there are more than 6 million videos on YouTube and the amount of time people have spent the site since it launched last year adds up to 9,305 years. Which means not only do you have a huge audience, it's also a highly engaged one.

So, how do you leverage YouTube for your brand? First, consider whether you want to go with one of the packaged YouTube offerings it just announced (http://www.clickz.com/showPage.html?page=3623233) or take a grass-roots approach.

When you consider YouTube, be prepared to break out of the way you've traditionally approached advertising, offline and on-. "This new medium requires finding a balance between traditional online advertising and new creative approaches that engage consumers in an active way," says Chad Hurley, CEO and cofounder of YouTube. "Advertisers now have a highly targeted opportunity for aligning their brands alongside the entertainment experience people are enjoying on YouTube."

Participatory Video Ads

The new Participatory Video Ad (PVA) is a user-initiated video advertisement with all the YouTube community features enabled. Consumers can rate, share, comment, embed, and add as a favorite advertising content. Rather than interrupt a consumer's experience, YouTube feels it's created a model that encourages engagement and participation.

The example I saw was a trailer for the movie "Crank." User comments varied from praise for the trailer and excitement about the movie to negative opinions about the trailer and the commercialization of YouTube. If you go this route, be prepared for the good and the bad user participation brings with it.

Brand Channels

Brand Channels include all standard community functionality, helping brands become an organic part of the YouTube's fabric. Key aspects include:

- Customized channel appearance through a self-service tool. Access to the enhanced design and channel functionality is free to advertisers who meet predetermined spending levels.

- Special promotional and media opportunities to help engage users with channel and video content.

- YouTube "Subscriptions." When a brand adds new videos to its channel, subscribers are notified, helping build audience.

- An autoplay video on the main channel page.

- Ability to host contests and encourage users to submit their own content.

I viewed the Paris Hilton channel, which I didn't find too interesting. It was sponsored by Fox's TV show "Prison Break." That's not to say a Brand Channel couldn't work, just that I see a disconnect between Paris Hilton and "Prison Break."

Grass-Root Approaches

There are unofficial approaches you can consider, too. Recently, Stephen Colbert of Comedy Central's "The Colbert Report" issued a challenge to his audience. He shot a video of himself on a green

YouTube

screen for fans to download and edit in any way they wanted. He asked people to submit the videos to his fan site. Many of the videos have also shown up on YouTube. The result has been phenomenal. One video alone on YouTube has been viewed almost 700,000 times, as of this writing. Giving assets to consumers to make the brand their own is just another way to potentially get your brand on YouTube. But this, too, can be risky.

Some brands are simply uploading TV spots and seeing what happens. A couple of ads that have gained enormous popularity on the site are Volkswagen's Pimp My Auto spots and the Sony Bravia Bouncy Balls ad.

As I said a few weeks ago, advertising within social media isn't for everyone. You may have concerns about inappropriate content surrounding your brand. But it's worthwhile to at least explore how it might work for you. The audiences, and their levels of engagement, are hard to ignore.

YouTube

What Can YouTube Learn From Search?

YouTube. has not been generally associated with search, but stands poised to bring bring the key attributes of search marketing to a more traditional environment. If it succeeds, it will not only reap significant advertising revenue for itself, it will set the model for an entire media sector scrambling to find a way to replenish eroding marketer dollars and consumer engagement.

The TV industry is currently reeling from the shift in media budget to other media. A lack of advertising accountability (aka tracking), engagement (those pesky DVRs!) and flexibility (in terms of pricing, creative format, etc.) have marketers flocking to Web-based platforms–and search marketing, in particular.

YouTube has the opportunity to resurrect video advertising. Given its robust platform and its immense popularity, YouTube is uniquely positioned to introduce an ad offering that marries the best of the search world with the best of the TV world.

The Best of the Search World

Proactive Consumption–similar to search as we know it today, on YouTube, consumers proactively seek out content by keyword or by popularity (PageRank, anyone?) All content is available on demand, and is consumed actively as opposed to passively. Advertising in this environment can and should be targeted, based on what we know about the user from his or her search. It should also be user-initiated and non-interruptive–keeping the consumer in control.

Mass Customization–with search, every ad can be customized based on what we know the consumer is looking for or has looked for in the past. On YouTube, each ad can and should be targeted, based on a query or past viewing behavior. It's unlike traditional TV, in which every person watching a particular channel at a particular time is exposed to the same ad.

Instant Point-of-Need Direction–typically, with search, a Web site is the destination a consumer is looking for, and marketers can point people to a page on their site that best meets their needs. However, this is changing–as evidenced by Google's moving its video link to its home page. More and more, consumers are looking for alternative forms of content. Now, instead of a Web site, a video can be the destination. And an ad in this environment can and should provide consumers with the ability to instantly take the next step–whether that is buying a product, downloading a coupon, finding a location, etc.

Dynamic Performance-Based Pricing–there's no question that the CPC auction model is one of the key drivers behind the rapid proliferation of search marketing. This pricing model brought a level of flexibility and accountability that was previously nonexistent in advertising. Hopefully, YouTube can resist the pressure to price its ad units on a CPM basis to align with traditional TV GRPs. No question–it will be hard for YouTube to pass up the "guaranteed" revenue that CPM pricing provides. Especially given the fact that it has millions of dollars in hosting fees to pay each month, and as yet, no significant revenue stream. However, with YouTube's massive scale and long tail — 20 million monthly unique users and 100 million DAILY video views–an auction CPC model is likely its best long-term option for maximum inventory monetization.

Alas, for all its strong features, search marketing does lack some vital attributes of the TV ad environment.

The Best of the TV World

Sight, Sound, and Motion–these three words have been the crutch of every brand marketer that ever resisted allocating budget to search. There's no question that it's easier to convey core brand attributes and resonate with consumers through video versus 95 characters of text. *Scale*–for mass marketers that want to reach vast audiences, the reach of TV is unparalleled. Currently TV reaches 111 million US households — about double the amount of people using search engines on a daily basis. While YouTube has nowhere near that kind of reach, it could one day, as new products like iTV from Apple bring online video to television.

The Best of the YouTube World

Passionate Audience–one aspect of social media that's truly unique is the forum it creates for audience participation. YouTube's slogan, "Broadcast Yourself," embodies the environment it has created. For whatever reason, part of this "expression" seems to be a resistance to all things "corporate"–advertising included. However, Google was in a similar position back in the day. It had a loyal, viral audience that it was scared of alienating with advertising. Nonetheless, it was able to win over consumers by providing ads that actually added value without interrupting the user-experience.

Passionate Contributors–what about the people producing the videos? Just like content publishers share in revenue via Google AdWords or AdSense distribution, so, too, should video producers get a piece of the action from YouTube. This would certainly encourage greater volume and quality of submissions. YouTube appears to have embraced the concept of revenue sharing, recently announcing a deal with Warner Music. How long before it creates a framework for all content producers–large and small–to profit?

Participatory Advertising – YouTube recently announced the launch of its first two ad concepts – Participatory Video Ads (PVAs) and Brand Channels. PVAs are user-initiated, and incorporate user-feedback to encourage engagement. Could user ratings be the first step towards a Google-like Quality Score? And Brand Channels feature a self-service interface for marketers to adjust their placements themselves. Can tools for auto-optimization be far behind?

Now, by no means do these initial ad formats represent the perfect union of search marketing and TV advertising. But they are a step in the right direction – at least You Tube's not going to market with pre- and post-rolls.

With the pressure mounting for it to start making money, let's hope YouTube can stay the course and continue to roll out advertising products that draw from the success of search marketing. If it does, it won't be long before the traditional media world shifts from trying to guess Google's next move to thinking WWYTD?

How To Make Money Embracing YouTube

I know it seems sexy right now for folks to comment on how you should let the community download and post music, videos, etc on social network sites like YouTube, MySpace, and etc for free. However, I keep asking questions on how these companies, bands, etc make money in the long term and how they recoup their investment. Every time I post a comment on expert sites I get similar answers like: don't wreck the community, these are big companies they'll make it up elsewhere, the classic Digital Millennium Copyright Act reply, or my favorite which is silence. One thing is clear that going after the end-user who posts the content is wrong because at the end of the day, they make nothing off of it and after all this is about money right?

You know how you make money if you are a major content owner? Embrace the community and cut deals with as many social networks as possible. That way, you get paid advertising and let the social networking shells work their magic with traffic, commentary, and friend building. You know like CBS is doing with YouTube.

It seems that after this deal has been in place which includes a CBS Channel on YouTube, CBS has seen awesome online as well as offline results. CBS is averaging over 850,000 views per day and have seen TV ratings boosted on Letterman as well as The Late, Late Show.

For a detailed look at the numbers, check out this press release (http://www.youtube.com/press_room_entry?entry=oJpEXVevcKg)

found over at YouTube - those are some nice views. The only problem right now with the CBS Channel on YouTube is the lack of enough advertising units to generate money (preroll video) and I'm not talking Google AdSense. The other disappointing piece of the press release is a lack of more concrete numbers - for example, when I've reported numbers for online videos I report minutes viewed and average time spent in the unit, not just viewership....no reason why the internet can't do better than counting views.

See, embracing the community while making money and protecting your copyrights can all be accomplished at the same time. All it takes is a little deal-cutting, cooler heads, and a realization that this is the world shaping up in front of us. To ignore the online video wave is like putting your head in the sand when Google's stock came out at $90.

YouTube Announces CBS Channel

Yet another new YouTube deal is struck. The video sharing site just announced an agreement with CBS to offer news, sports and entertainment clips on a daily basis, kicking off this month. YouTube and CBS will share revenue from the sponsorship of CBS Videos. Content set to appear includes "Survivor", "CSI" and "The Late Show with Dave Letterman", all from CBS Entertainment. The news division, meanwhile, will serve up "CBS Evening News with Katie Couric", "The Early Show" and "60 Minutes." There'll be sports content from CBS Sports, and Showtime Networks will supply trailers from "Dexter", "Brotherhood", "Sleeper Cell and "The L Word".

The deal also includes content from CSTV, the college athletics channel. Although YouTube haven't announced a tie-up between YouTube Colleges and CSTV, it's certainly possible. They want to encourage university students to upload content from tailgate parties and pep rallies - YouTube Colleges gives direct access to that demographic.

What's more, CBS will be the first to test YouTube's new "content identification architecture", which allows the company to track down unauthorized use of their copyrighted content - CBS will then have the choice to remove the clips, or let them stay up. But here's the interesting bit: if they decide not to remove unauthorized content, YouTube will share the revenue from any ads placed around those clips. In other words: YouTube is now incentivizing the TV companies to leave their content on the site, even if a user put it there without permission. This is the ideal solution to the copyright problem, and I sincerely hope it works out.

The move comes straight after the launch of DiddyTV, the P. Diddy Channel, and other TV and music deals including the NBC-YouTube hookup and an agreement with Warner Music. As the deals keep piling up, it looks more and more likely that the content companies are going to play ball, rather than suing. Even so, legal action is still a real possibility.

Update: YouTube also just announced deals with Sony BMG and Universal Music. Ironic, since it was Universal that said "MySpace and YouTube Owe Us Millions". Still, it looks like another potential court case has been avoided. See also my last post on Google Video's deals with the same companies.

AFTER ONE MONTH, CBS CONTENT AMONG MOST VIEWED VIDEOS ON YOUTUBE

Nearly 30 Million Views Since Partnership Began Oct. 18

NEW YORK, NY and SAN BRUNO, Calif. — One month after launching the CBS Brand Channel on YouTube, CBS's daily feed of news, sports and entertainment clips have become some of the most widely viewed content on the site.

CBS has uploaded more than 300 clips that have a total of 29.2 million views on YouTube, averaging 857,000 views per day, since the service launched on October 18. CBS has three of the top 25 most viewed videos this month (Nov.1–17), including clips from CBS's Tuesday night hit drama "NCIS," "Late Show with David Letterman," "The Late Late Show with Craig Ferguson" and "The Early Show." The CBS Brand Channel is also one of the most subscribed channels of all time with more than 20,000 users subscribing to CBS programming on YouTube since the channel launch last month.

"Above all the other good news, what's most exciting here is the extent to which CBS is learning about its audience as never before," said Quincy Smith, President, CBS Interactive. "YouTube users are clearly being entertained by the CBS programming they're watching as evidenced by the sheer number of video views. Professional content seeds YouTube and allows an open dialogue between established media players and a new set of viewers. We believe this inflection point is the precursor to many exciting developments as we continue to build bridges rather than construct walls."

"CBS has done a phenomenal job at engaging and interacting with the YouTube community and we're pleased that this has brought new viewers to their broadcasts. It's been great watching our community respond so strongly and positively to their entertaining content," said Kevin Donahue, Vice President of Content for YouTube. "We look forward to working with CBS to help them promote their quality programming while bringing timely video content to our user community."

Ratings for the network's late night programs, in particular, have shown notable increases. CBS's "Late Show with David Letterman" has added 200,000 (+5%) new viewers while "The Late Late Show with Craig Ferguson" is up 100,000 viewers (+7%) since the YouTube postings started. Although the success of these shows on YouTube is not the sole cause of the rise in television ratings, both companies believe that YouTube has brought a significant new audience of viewers to each broadcast.

Here are the Top 15 CBS videos watched (as of Nov. 17 2006):

Title

1. NCIS/Cat Fight

Total Views: 1,603,364

http://www.youtube.com/watch?v=DowFLyuHaeo

2. Letterman/ Borat Meets David Letterman

Total Views: 1,057,180

http://www.youtube.com/watch?v=NvQScRuZj9s

3. Early Show/ Borat Vs Harry Smith

Total Views: 969,391

http://www.youtube.com/watch?v=UnbnaT8If0Q

4. Letterman/ Bush is drinking again

Total Views: 698,806

http://www.youtube.com/watch?v=irOFAjsnSg0

5. Letterman/ Message About February for Bush

Total Views: 524,697

http://www.youtube.com/watch?v=NmX23l0ouo8

6. CBS Evening News/ Michael J Fox Talks to Katie Couric

Total Views: 465,563

http://www.youtube.com/watch?v=o8lsjfjgAA8

7. CSTV/USC Cheerleaders: The Song Girls

Total Views: 374,623

http://www.youtube.com/watch?v=8KtR2oeXFqo

8. CSTV/ A Field of Dreams for Judy Coffman

Total View: 358,572

http://www.youtube.com/watch?v=IWERvnzVkYE

9. Letterman/George W. Bush Fakin' It

Total Views: 357,213

http://www.youtube.com/watch?v=cVOj6iP_iVs

10. Letterman/ Dave and Bill O'Reilly

Total View: 352,747

http://www.youtube.com/watch?v=d0nD_iNPalY

11. Letterman/The Guy Who Swears At Dave

Total Views: 316,258

http://www.youtube.com/watch?v=foyLyriak-Q

12. Ferguson/ Fun is Dangerous

Total Views: 314,093

http://www.youtube.com/watch?v=jFMfmXWlAGs

13. Letterman/Do Maggots Go With Scorpion

YouTube

Total Views: 278,283

http://www.youtube.com/watch?v=Jjed2Xq0ImI

14. Ferguson/ Bush visits the Un-Late Late Show

Total Views: 221,462

http://www.youtube.com/watch?v=5fvqMF34iG4

15. Ferguson/Bad Kerry

Total Views: 219,556

http://www.youtube.com/watch?v=M6Bz_r5CZTk

CBS and YouTube launched the CBS Brand Channel in October, which included clips from "Late Show with Dave Letterman," "The Late Late Show with Craig Ferguson," "NCIS" and "CSI: Miami," as well as archival sports footage such as great finishes and upsets from NCAA's March Madness. CBS has also provided clips from "CBS News First Look with Katie Couric," in which Couric offers a web-exclusive rundown of the stories being considered for coverage on that night's "CBS Evening News." "First Look" also offers some perspective on what is going on in the world that day.

About CBS CBS Corporation (NYSE: CBS.A and CBS) is a mass media company with constituent parts that reach back to the beginnings of the broadcast industry, as well as newer businesses that operate on the leading edge of the media industry. The

Company, through its many and varied operations, combines broad reach with well-positioned local businesses, all of which provide it with an extensive distribution network by which it serves audiences and advertisers in all 50 states and key international markets. It has operations in virtually every field of media and entertainment, including broadcast television (CBS and The CW – a joint venture between CBS Corporation and Warner Bros. Entertainment), cable television (Showtime and CSTV Networks), local television (CBS Television Stations), television production and syndication (CBS Paramount Network Television and CBS Television Distribution Group), radio (CBS Radio), advertising on out-of-home media (CBS Outdoor), publishing (Simon & Schuster), digital media (CBS Interactive and CSTV Networks) and consumer products (CBS Consumer Products). For more information, log on to www.cbscorporation.com.

What Your Business Can Learn From YouTube

The reason why YouTube, Wikipedia, and other user generated content sites are big is because of the elements contained in them.

These elements can be implemented in your own business tomorrow. Here they are

Element number one is user generated. (**Example:** YouTube, Wikipedia.) Would you break something that you have created? Would you say anything bad about what you've been a part of? If you contribute to something wouldn't it become more important to you? (Ok, enough with the questions)

The main point is we feel attached to things we create or contribute to. When people are in no way attached to your business idea, content, lead or profit they are less passionate about it. Pretty much they don't care about you. So why should they buy from you? Don't answer that.

How to apply this to your business? - Have a section on your site where content can be generated by visitors (customers). How about a blog with guest articles? How about Success stories by customers? Let your customers share how your company made their lives better.

Element number two is sense of community. (**Example:** BuildABear, Harley-Davidson, Volkswagen). If they contribute and others do the same it creates a "community like feel", that most people enjoy when it's relevant to them. People want to be a part of something that's bigger than them. They want to feel needed and important to others. It's in human needs to be attached to something that will make them feel this way.

Every kid that built that bear at Buildabear company knows that he/she is part of the group of other kids who have their personal bear. Every Harley-Davidson owner knows that he/she is a part of that huge community. Hey, these guys have shows and events just for them. Take Volkswagen huge, huge owners club.

How to apply this to your business tomorrow? - Add a public forum to your site? A message board. Just like the previous element, let your customers and fans share the "love" and "joy". This will get your future customers excited and motivated to join the community.

The bottom line here is remove that wall that people can usually see between the consumer and the company. It's not surprising how companies such as YouTube, NetFlix, Starbucks, BuildABear, JetBlue and many more grew so quickly with a huge loyal fan base.

Here Are TWO Ways To Make Money Off YouTube And GOOGLE Video

There are actually many ways to make extra money off You Tube and Google.

Here are just 2.

1. You can create a homemade video on whatever topic you know something about. Something about brushing cats or something to that effect.

You give a 2 minute *teaser* in the video explaining a few details on brushing the cat. You then mention in the video or that you have the full video for sale (for more information they can go to your website or ebay auction) where they can purchase the full 30-60 minute version of whatever topic you chose.

2.Did you know you can already use Google Video and You Tube videos that are already online? Google and You Tube will give you the codes to place those videos on any website. You can actually choose a topic. Create a website on that topic. Place the Google Video or You Tube code on that topicand then place affiliate links or Google Adsense around that topic. People will click on the video and then click on the links that talk about your topic. You would be surprised on how much money you make doing that.

It's Time to Learn About YouTube

Probably the world can be divided in our time between people who really know what YouTube is and people who don't. No need to be embarrassed if you're clueless about YouTube. It's hard to keep up. That's because there is one fact no one will ever challenge: The earth still spins on its axis every 24 hours, and work and sleep own most of them. Thus we may posit an iron law of the universe: You can do whatever it is you choose to do with your few free hours, or you can spend them with YouTube.

Millions prefer YouTube. So on Monday Google bought it for $1.65 billion. Should you care? I think so.

YouTube.com is a Web site. It entered the World Wide Web in February 2005 with a homepage that said: "YouTube: Broadcast Yourself." The site's technology lets people create a personal channel and then upload video to it for everyone to see. That's pretty much it. Why is this worth $1.65 billion and your idea isn't? Because every day 65,000 new videos are uploaded to YouTube's site, and every day the world's people tune into 100 million of these videos. One consultant with time on his hands has calculated that during YouTube's short life, people have spent 9,305 years watching it.

A cynic would say YouTube's home-video billions proves investors would put money in people watching ice melt if the numbers added up. Well, there are at least 15 videos on YouTube that let you watch ice melting, including one of a group of Japanese rubbing a block of ice to get at the coins inside. My own instinct at the news of Google's big buy was to mock YouTube. Put it this way: The five American scientists who just won Nobel Prizes probably haven't, nor would they, spend five seconds on YouTube. But then I paddled my surfboard onto the Web site over a few days. It may not be long before the Nobelists arrive with videos.

The politicians have already landed. The good news is this means they won't strangle YouTube in its crib with legislation. The bad news is the politicians' own videos, or those of their proxies, may give the site a worse name than the thousands uploading videos of cats playing Bach and similar whimsies.

News articles have begun to appear noting that some campaigns are uploading videos to YouTube. The campaigns hire someone with a camcorder to follow an opponent, film the candidate constantly and post embarrassing moments on YouTube.

Sen. George Allen was famously caught calling his camcorder stalker a "macaca." Then there is "Conrad Burns' Naptime," which has had 80,000 views and was put up by his opponent Jon Tester. Or "Rick Santorum Throws a Tantrum," posted by SantorumExposed, with 57,000 views. In fact, Sen. Burns is fighting sleep at a committee hearing, which is unremarkable, and Sen. Santorum didn't throw a tantrum, but simply argued with a woman about taxes while walking on a street. This is essentially the embarrassing technique Michael Moore used at the opening of "Fahrenheit 9/11," catching people in a weak moment.

So the new-media types discovered YouTube and rode its potential straight to the bottom. If the weak-moment tactic catches on, it will of course drive what's left of normal people out of politics. More ironic is that the explicit goal of the YouTube political sites is to attract the attention of mainstream-media reporters for print and TV, which is the only way these videos can gain traction. Search YouTube for video of the Montana debate between Sen. Burns and Jon Tester. Number of views? A few hundred.

Political videos are just a blip in the vast YouTube ocean. The power of this site is simply the power of the moving picture, a force not fully understood since Edison unleashed it. Like Google, the mother of all search engines, YouTube is a town square where the locals come to find out things, or now with YouTube, see something--anything.

It is easy to imagine YouTube (or a competitor's site if YouTube blows it) becoming the repository for most of the world's moving images. The amateur archivists are already there, finally able to share their collections with everyone. I typed in "Thelonious Monk." Instantly, I was watching Monk play "Round Midnight" in Europe in 1964. It is mesmerizing. Then I watched Keith Jarrett solo in Tokyo in 1984; Chet Baker, Bill Evans, Barney Kessel; Duke Ellington playing "C-Jam Blues" in 1942, John Coltrane with Miles Davis, Arthur Rubinstein, Glenn Gould discussing Bach fugues, Andres Segovia. This was the video experience of visiting the Morgan Library in New York and looking at famous writers' original manuscripts.

The list of attendant issues and problems raised is endless, not least copyright. Or the even more powerful new ethos that it all has to be "free."

It would be awful, though, if whatever is going on here was driven underground. This isn't Grokster, where virtually the whole game was "steal this song." There is a weird, naive innocence about much of YouTube now. A lot of the videos on YouTube remind me of the garage bands and living room doo-wop groups of the 1950s. There is a widely viewed video of a young Korean guitarist named "funtwo," sitting on his bed and playing a rock version of Pachelbel's Canon with eye-popping skill.

Do I wish more people chose to spend some of life's precious free hours listening to Ian McKellan's reading of Robert Fagels's translation of the Odyssey? Yes, but maybe the publisher should put up a 10-minute clip of Mr. McKellan doing exactly that to drive buyers to it. And rather than just trudge cross-country to readings at

YouTube

endless Barnes & Nobles, might not authors also present their work and ideas in person on YouTube? (Though not 'til Google gives its partner a decent search function.) Even a Nobelist might wish to explain his brilliance to a wider audience than he'll get in Oslo. Stand up a camcorder and start talking.

In keeping with the times, YouTubers try not to waste yours. Most clips run under five minutes. Guess they have other things to do.

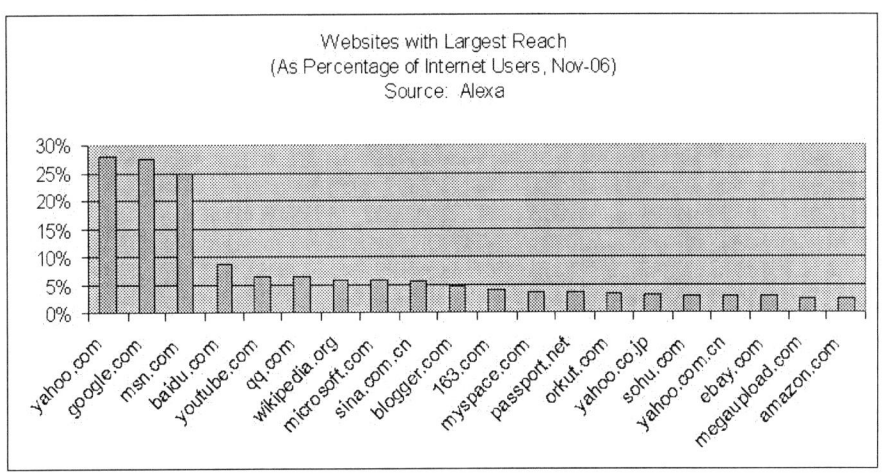

YouTube

YouTube

YouTube

YouTube

YouTube

YouTube

LEARNING VIDEO SHARING WITH YOUTUBE

Getting Started

General Questions About YouTube

What is YouTube?

YouTube is an online video streaming service that allows anyone to view and share videos that have been uploaded by our members.

How do videos get featured?

YouTube's members rate videos they like, and we review highly-rated and recent videos for consideration in the "Featured Videos" section of the home page and the featured videos on the "Categories" page. In addition, our programming team takes suggestions from members at editor@youtube.com and scans the site for videos of interest.

What is TestTube?

TestTube (http://www.youtube.com/testtube) is an area of the site where we try out new features to get feedback from users before they're officially launched.

Signing Up

How do I join?

To become a member of YouTube, go to the "Signup" page (http://www.youtube.com/signup), choose a user name and password, and enter your information. Then click the "Sign Up" button and you're done.

How do I confirm my email address?

Confirming your email address is required to perform many actions on YouTube, such as uploading videos and posting comments. It is now part of signing up for new members, but if you signed up prior to February 2007 and have not yet confirmed your email address, follow these steps:

1. Go to the Confirm Email page (http://www.youtube.com/email_confirm).
2. Enter the email addresss you would like to use as your contact for YouTube. Please enter the email address you used when you joined.
3. Click the "Submit" button.
4. Check your email for a message from YouTube and click the link in the email to complete the confirmation process.

If you don't receive the confirmation email within a few minutes, be sure to check your spam folder to make sure it wasn't misfiled.

I keep being told the username I want is taken. How do I find a user name that works?

YouTube has experienced a lot of growth in user numbers. As a result, you may need to get a little more creative with your user name selection. Try adding other characters before or after the user name you wish to use—many people add their birth year or other identifying information, like this: Maria1972, MariaNY. You can also bracket the name with other characters like this: xxUSERxx.

You can only use letters and numbers for your user name; no spaces or special characters like dashes or underscores are allowed. User names are not case-sensitive, so 123ABC will be recognized as the same as 123abc. Therefore, if someone else has the user name you want but capitalizes different letters than you, you still can't create that user name.

Solving Sign-up and Log-in Issues

I keep being asked to log in, even though I entered my username and password correctly. What should I do?

If you are unable to login with what you know to be your correct username and password, please ensure that you have cookies enabled. If your cookies are already enabled or enabling them doesn't resolve this issue, try the second process below: Clearing the browser's cache.

Enabling cookies

To find out how to enable cookies, click your browser:

- Internet Explorer 7
- Internet Explorer 6
- Firefox 2.x (PC)
- Firefox 1.x (PC)
- Firefox (Mac)
- Safari

Enable cookies for Internet Explorer 7

1. Click "Start" and select "Control Panel".
   (Note: With Windows XP Classic View, click the Windows "Start" button, then select "Settings" and "Control Panel").
2. Open the Internet Options icon.
3. Choose the "Privacy" tab.
4. Click the "Advanced" button.
5. Check the box "Override automatic cookie handling" under the Cookies section in the Advanced Privacy Settings window.
6. Under First-party Cookies, select the "Accept" or "Prompt" option.

7. Under Third-party Cookies, select the "Accept" or "Prompt" option.
(Note: If you select the "Prompt" option you will be prompted every time a Web site attempts to send you a cookie to click "OK".)
8. In the Internet Options window, click "OK" to exit.
9. If this doesn't solve the issue, try: Clear the cache for Internet Explorer 7.

Enable cookies for Internet Explorer 6

1. Click "Start" and select "Control Panel".

   (Note: With Windows XP Classic View, click the Windows "Start" button and select "Settings" and "Control Panel")

2. Select the "Privacy" tab.
3. Click the "Advanced" button.
4. Place a check in the "Override Automatic Cookie Handling" check box.
5. Under First Party Cookies, select the "Accept" or "Prompt" option.
6. Under Third Party Cookies, select the "Accept" or "Prompt" option.

   (Note: If you select the "Prompt" option you will be prompted every time a Web site attempts to send you a cookie to click "OK".)

7. In the Internet Options window, click "OK" to exit.
8. If this doesn't solve the issue, try: Clear the cache for Internet Explorer 6.

YouTube

Enable cookies for Mozilla Firefox 2.x (PC)

1. In Mozilla Firefox, select "Tools" from the file menu.
2. Select "Options".
3. Click on the "Privacy" icon in the top panel.
4. Check the box corresponding to "Accept cookies from sites".
5. Click "OK" to save and close.
6. If this doesn't solve the issue, try: Clear the cache for Firefox 2.x (PC).

Enable cookies for Mozilla Firefox 1.x (PC)

1. In Mozilla Firefox, select "Tools" from the file menu.
2. Select "Options".
3. Click on the "Privacy" icon in the top panel.
4. Click on the "Cookies" tab.
5. Check the "Allow sites to set cookies" checkbox.
6. Click "OK" to save and close.
7. If this doesn't solve the issue, try: Clear the cache for Firefox 1.x (PC).

Enable cookies for Mozilla Firefox (Mac)

1. Go to the "Firefox" drop down menu.
2. Select "Preferences".
3. Select the "Privacy" icon.
4. Under "Cookies", mark the checkbox for "Allow sites to set Cookies".
5. If this doesn't solve the issue, try: Clear the cache for Firefox (Mac).

YouTube

Enable cookies for Safari

1. Go to the "Safari" drop down menu.
2. Select "Preferences".
3. Select the "Security" icon at the top panel.
4. Under "Accept Cookies" section select "Only from sites you navigate to".
5. If this doesn't solve the issue, try: Clear the cache for Safari.

Clearing the browser's cache

If your cookies were already enabled or enabling cookies doesn't resolve the problem, you may also want to clear the cookies that are stored on your computer (Please note that while clearing your cookies may resolve the problem, it will also remove your saved settings for sites you've previously visited.)

To find out how to clear the cache, click your browser:

- Internet Explorer 7
- Internet Explorer 6
- Firefox 2.x (PC)
- Firefox 1.x (PC)
- Firefox (Mac)
- Safari

Clear the cache for Internet Explorer 7

1. Click "Start" and select "Control Panel".
   (Note: With Windows XP Classic View click the Windows "Start" button and select "Settings" and "Control Panel").
2. Open the "Internet Options" icon.
3. Click on the "General" tab if it isn't selected already.
4. Under the Browsing history section, click the "Delete..." button.
5. Click the "Delete cookies..." button.

6. Select "Yes" if a box appears to confirm.
7. Click "OK" to close the window.

Clear the cache for Internet Explorer 6

1. Click "Start" and select "Control Panel".
   (Note: Windows XP Classic View click the Windows "Start" button and select "Settings" and "Control Panel")
2. Open the "Internet Options" icon.
3. Click on the "General" tab if it isn't selected already.
4. Under the heading "Temporary Internet files," click the "Delete Cookies..." button.
5. Click "OK" for the "Delete all cookies in the Temporary Internet Files folder?" prompt.
6. Click "OK" to exit.

Clear the cache for Mozilla Firefox 2.x (PC)

1. In Mozilla Firefox, select "Tools" from the file menu.
2. Select "Options".
3. Under the "Private Data" heading, click the "Clear Now" button.
4. Click "OK" to exit.

Clear the cache for Mozilla Firefox 1.x (PC)

1. In Mozilla Firefox, select "Tools" from the file menu.
2. Select "Options".
3. Click on the "Privacy" icon in the top panel.
4. Click on the "Cookies" tab.
5. Check the "Clear Cookies Now" button.
6. Click "OK" to save and close.

YouTube

Clear the cache for Mozilla Firefox (Mac)

1. Go to the "Firefox" drop down menu.
2. Select "Preferences."
3. Select the "Privacy" icon.
4. In version 1.5, click "Clear Cache Now." In 1.0, next to "Cache," click the "Clear" button, and then "OK." In 2.0, click on the "Clear Now" button under the "Private Data" heading.

Clear the cache for Safari

1. Go to the "Safari" drop down menu.
2. Select "Preferences".
3. Select the "Security" icon at the top panel.
4. From the Security dialog box, click "Bookmarks".
5. Click "Show Cookies".
6. From the Cookie dialog box, click to choose cookies from youtube.com, and click "Remove". Alternatively, if you want to delete all cookies, click "Remove All".
7. Click "Done".

I forgot my user name or password. How do I log back into the site?

If you forgot your password, you can retrieve it here (http://www.youtube.com/forgot).

If you forgot your user name, you can retrieve it here (http://www.youtube.com/forgot_username).

The verification code will not accept.

When you sign up to become a YouTube member, the verification code may sometimes produce color combinations that make it hard for people with colorblindness to correctly discern the characters. If you're having trouble, try clicking the "Can't read?" link under the verification code box. This will change the color combination. If you continue to have trouble, you may want to ask a friend to help confirm the code being displayed.

I never received my confirmation email. What happened?

If you have just joined YouTube, the confirmation link is included in the "Welcome" email you received after signing up. If you were already a member of YouTube and are now confirming your email, you will receive a separate confirmation email.

If you don't receive either the welcome or confirmation email when you expect to, check in your email client's spam folder—some are more aggressive than others about identifying spam. If you still haven't received it after several hours, you can try confirming your email again with a different email address by returning to the "Upload" page (http://www.youtube.com/my_videos_upload).

Watching Videos

BROWSING THE SITE

How do I find my uploaded videos?

In the upper right corner of most pages, you'll find a line of links to all of your stuff: videos, favorites, playlists, inbox, and subscriptions.

If you're on a page that doesn't have this bar (such as a video watch page), you can get to your videos by clicking the "My Account" link at the top of the page and then clicking the "My Uploaded Videos" link.

Or you can go directly to your videos (http://www.youtube.com/my_videos).

How do I find cool videos to watch?

There are lots of ways to find cool videos to watch. Here are four to start with:

- If you know what you're looking for, you can type keywords into the Search box at the top of every page.

- Click on the Videos tab to browse the site; the links across the top give you an idea of what other folks on YouTube find interesting, and you can dig deeper within each one using the Time, Category, and Language links on the left to refine the list of videos.

- You can also browse the site from the Categories tab to find videos in a more specific area (for example, Pets or Comedy), and refine the list from there using the Search box within the category.

- When you find other members whose videos you like, you can subscribe to them so that you're notified whenever they upload new videos—the newest four will show up on the home page when you login, or you can view all of your subscriptions to see them all at once.

How do I get back to a video I watched a couple of minutes ago?

At the top right corner of each page is a line of utility links. Click the "History" link to see your Viewing History since you opened the browser. This list is cleared out every time you quit the browser, so if there are videos you want to save to watch later, save them to your Favorites or to a Playlist.

Go directly to your Viewing History

How do I clear my Viewing History?

At the top right corner of each page is a line of utility links. Click the 'History' link to see your Viewing History. To clear it, click the 'Clear Viewing History' link at the bottom of the video list. The Viewing History will also be cleared automatically when you quit the browser.

Go directly to your Viewing History

SEARCHING FOR VIDEOS

Why isn't my video showing up in search?

Depending on site traffic, changes to video information can take 8 hours or more to show up in the search index after they have been uploaded, changed, or removed. This includes changes to tags, ratings, views, and comments. Under extreme site traffic we have seen some videos take over 24 hours to index. To bypass this time you may want to send your friends the link of the video via email or private message.

Note that unless the user name of the uploader is specified as a tag it may not be indexed for a video search. To find a user (and their videos) perform a search for their user name select "Channels" on the left side of the search results.

How do I search for a Playlist?

To find a Playlist, enter your search terms in the Search box at the top or bottom of each page. When you get to the search results page, click the "Playlists" link on the left side of the page to search Playlists specifically.

Do you save my search history?

No. YouTube doesn't save your searches, but your browser probably does. If you don't want to see your previous search terms displayed in the search field, you need to clear the search history in your browser.

Is there a SafeSearch option?

YouTube doesn't currently have a SafeSearch option.

Saving, Collecting, and Sharing Videos

SAVING VIDEOS

Can I download videos to watch later?

No, currently you can't download our videos to your computer. YouTube's video player is designed to be used within your browser as an Internet experience. As an alternative to downloading, you can temporarily save videos to watch later by adding them to your QuickList. If you'd like to save them more permanently, login and click "Save to Favorites" under the videos you'd like to keep.

How do I watch and save videos?

Watching videos on YouTube couldn't be easier—just come to the site and browse around, or search for subjects that interest you. To save videos permanently, you need to sign up as a member, and then click the "Save to Favorites" link underneath the videos you want to watch later. You can also use the QuickList feature to save videos temporarily; they will disappear from the list when you quit your browser.

What is a QuickList and how do I use it?

QuickList is a way to make a list of videos to watch later in your session. To add videos to your list, just click the "+" on any video you'd like to save. Once your list is created, you can see the QuickList bar under any video you watch. Click the down arrow to display the full bar, and you can skip around in your list or just click "Play All" to watch them all in sequence.

YouTube

If you haven't made a QuickList yet, you can <u>look at the tutorial</u> (http://www.youtube.com/watch_queue) to see how.

COLLECTING VIDEOS INTO PLAYLISTS

How do I search for a Playlist?

To find a Playlist, enter your search terms in the Search box at the top or bottom of each page. When you get to the search results page, click the "Playlists" link on the left side of the page to search Playlists specifically.

What is a Playlist?

Playlists are collections of videos that can be watched on YouTube, shared with other people, or embedded into websites or blogs. "Favorites" is your default Playlist, but you can create as many as you want.

How do I make a Playlist?

There are several ways to make Playlists.

From the video watch page:

1. Click on the "Save to Favorites" link under the video you're watching.
2. From the dropdown menu, choose "[New Playlist]", and click "OK." You'll be taken to a page where you can set the properties for your Playlist.
3. Click the "Save Playlist Info" button. You'll be returned to the video watch page and the video will automatically be added to your new Playlist.

From your QuickList:

1. Go to the "QuickList" page (http://www.youtube.com/watch_queue).
2. Remove any videos that you don't want to have in your Playlist
3. Click the "Save as Playlist" link at the bottom of the video list.

From your Account:

1. Go to your Playlists directly by clicking the "Playlists" link near the top right of most pages, or go to the "My Account" page (http://www.youtube.com/my_account) and click on the "Playlists" link in the "Videos" section.
2. Click the "Create Playlist" button and set the properties for your Playlist.
3. Click the "Save Playlist Info" button. You'll be returned to the "My Playlists" page and can begin adding video

How do I share a Playlist?

1. Go to the "My Playlists" page (http://www.youtube.com/my_playlists).
2. Click on the link of the playlist you want to share.
3. In the blue bar at the top, click the "Share this Playlist" link.
4. Enter the email addresses (or usernames, if you're logged in) of the people with whom you'd like to share the Playlist.
5. Click the "Send" button.

What's the difference between a Playlist and a QuickList?

Your QuickList is a temporary list of videos, which you can add to while you are browsing around the site. It will only exist until you quit your browser, and you can only have one QuickList at a time. Your QuickList can't be shared with other people.

Playlists are permanent collections of videos that you create. You can change the order of videos in a Playlist, share it with other people, and set it to appear in your Profile as a Vlog. You can have more than one Playlist, and can also embed them in your website or blog.

Your QuickList and Playlists can both be set to play all the videos they contain.

SHARING VIDEOS

How do I share videos?

Sharing a video is simple—just click on the "Share" button at the bottom of the video player, and enter the email addresses (or YouTube usernames, if you're logged in) of the people to whom you want to send it. Click the "Send" button, and you're all done!

How do I make my video private?

If you'd like to make sure your video(s) are seen only by the people you hand-pick, you should set your video to "Private". Here's how:

1. Log in and go to "My Videos" (http://youtube.com/my_videos).
2. Click the "Edit Video Info" button beside the video in question.
3. Scroll down to the Broadcast section and select the "Private" option.
4. Be sure to then select the specific contact list you want to see the video.
5. Always double-check to be sure the contact list you select includes only the people you want to see that video. Check your Contact Lists (http://youtube.com/my_friends).
6. Click the "Update Video Info" button.

How do I share a Playlist?

1. Go to the "My Playlists" page (http://www.youtube.com/my_playlists).
2. Click on the link of the playlist you want to share.
3. In the blue bar at the top, click the "Share this Playlist" link.
4. Enter the email addresses (or usernames, if you're logged in) of the people with whom you'd like to share the Playlist.
5. Click the "Send" button.

Can I embed or share a private video?

Yes. You can embed a private video on your website by copying the embed code on the "Edit Video" page for that video and pasting it into your website. To share it, just click the "Share Video" link under the video while you're watching it, and send it to whoever you like.

In order to view the video, the person coming to your website must be logged into YouTube, and be part of the list you shared the video with (i.e. Friends or Family). If they are not, the video will display "Loading," but the video will not load.

Who can see my private video?

When you make a video private, you have the option of sharing it with any of the lists you've created (you have two default lists, "Friends" and "Family"). If you don't select a list, your private video can only be viewed by your account. If you share it with a list, it will only be viewable by members on that list.

YouTube

WORKING WITH BLOGS

How do I embed videos on my website or blog?

To embed a video, just copy the code from the "Embed" box—you can find it in the "About This Video" box when you're watching the video.

You can also get the code from the "Embed HTML" box on the "Edit Video" page (http://www.youtube.com/my_videos_edit) if the video is yours. Once you've copied the code, just paste it into your website or blog to embed it.

For more information on embedding, you should check out our Sharing YouTube Videos page (http://youtube.com/sharing).

Can I make my embedded videos autoplay?

Yes, you can autoplay movies! In the "About This Video" section of the video watch page, we give you the source code to embed the video:

<object width="425" height="350"><param name="movie" value="http://www.youtube.com/v/OdT9z-JjtJk"></param><embed src="http://www.youtube.com/v/OdT9z-JjtJk" type="application/x-shockwave-flash" width="425" height="350"></embed></object>

To make it autoplay, just append "&autoplay=1" after the video ID so it looks like this:

<object width="425" height="350"><param name="movie" value="http://www.youtube.com/v/OdT9z-JjtJk**&autoplay=1**"></param><embed src="http://www.youtube.com/v/OdT9z-JjtJk**&autoplay=1**" type="application/x-shockwave-flash" width="425" height="350"></embed></object>

YouTube

How do I link to videos from my website or blog?

To link to a YouTube video, just copy the URL from your browser, and then paste it into your website or blog. Depending on the blogging or web design software you use, it may make the link clickable automatically. If it doesn't and you would like the link to be clickable, set it up like this, substituting your link for the YouTube link in quotes:

<a href="http://www.youtube.com/watch?v=xxxxxxxxxx">This cool video I found!</a>

How do I add a blog to my YouTube account?

To add a blog to your account, follow the steps below:

1. Click the "Video Posting Settings" link (http://www.youtube.com/my_profile_blogs) on your account page.
2. Click the "

Making, Uploading, and Promoting Videos

MAKING VIDEOS

How do I make or record a video?

You'll need to have a device that can capture digital movies—this could be a camcorder, digital camera, or even your cell phone! You copy the movies to your computer, and then you can either upload them as-is or edit them with software such as iMovie or Windows Movie Maker to add titles and special effects. For more detailed information, read the Making and Optimizing Your Videos guide (http://www.youtube.com/t/howto_makevideo).

For some types of cellphones and mobile devices, you can also upload to YouTube directly, without copying the file to your computer first.

Do I have to have a camcorder to make videos?

No. While camcorders are a great way to make videos, they aren't the only one. You can make videos with a webcam, digital camera, or even some cellphones.

How do I put videos from my mobile device onto YouTube?

If your phone has video and multimedia messaging (MMS) capabilities, you can probably upload videos from your cell phone or other mobile device. Here's how to set it up:

1. Log in to YouTube and go to the "My Account" page.
2. Under "Account Settings," click the "Mobile Upload Profiles" link.

YouTube

3. Click the "Create Mobile Profile" button and enter the information required.
4. Click the "Create Profile" button.

When your profile is set up, you will be given an email address similar to this: **1111111111@mms.youtube.com**. When you want to upload a video taken with your phone, email it to that address. After it's uploaded, you can go to YouTube and edit the information about the video if you want.

How do I use my webcam with YouTube?

There are two ways to use your webcam with YouTube. You can record video using the software that came with the camera, and then upload it to YouTube, with or without editing first. You can also record directly to YouTube using the QuickCapture feature.

What is QuickCapture and how do I use it?

QuickCapture is a way to record video directly into YouTube. You need to have a webcam or camcorder attached to your computer and a confirmed email address to use this feature. To record and upload video using QuickCapture:

1. Log in to YouTube. Make sure your camera is attached to the computer and working.
2. Go to the "Quick Capture" page (http://www.youtube.com/my_videos_quick_capture).
3. Enter the information about your video in the left column. This is required before you begin recording.
4. If you get a message that says "www.youtube.com is requesting access to your camera and microphone," click the "Allow" button.
5. If you don't see a picture in the record section, you may need to choose a different video source from the video dropdown in the "Record Video" window.

YouTube

6. Once you see a picture coming from your camera, click the "Record" button to start recording your video.
7. When you're finished recording, click the "Done" button if you're satisfied with your video, or click the "Re-Record" button if you'd like to try recording it again.

When you click the "Done" button, your video is automatically uploaded to YouTube and starts processing. You can edit information about the video by going to the "<u>My Videos</u>" page (http://www.youtube.com/my_videos).

EDITING AND EXPORTING VIDEOS

What video file formats can I upload?

YouTube accepts video files from most digital cameras, camcorders, and cell phones in the .WMV, .AVI, .MOV, and .MPG file formats.

What is an .MSWMM file?

A .MSWMM file is a Windows Movie Maker project file. By saving the project, it allows you to return to the movie and make modifications at a later time. However, if you're satisfied with the movie and would like to upload and share the result through YouTube, you will need to choose "Save Movie File" under the "File" menu (which is different from "Save Project", which creates the .MSWMM file).

How do I edit my video?

Most computers come with some sort of video editing application already installed, such as Apple iMovie or Microsoft Movie Maker. Using these programs, you can easily edit your videos, add soundtracks, change the file type, compress the file size, etc.

There are also more advanced editing programs available for purchase or download online. We encourage you to look around and find the editing software that's right for you.

What is an .mov file?

Files saved with a .mov extension are QuickTime movies. They are often created by iMovie on a Mac, but other video editing programs can also save in this format. QuickTime .mov files can be uploaded to YouTube without any additional conversion.

YouTube

How do I change the audio track in my video?

Want to turn your masterpiece into a music video? Ready to refresh your soundtrack? YouTube now offers a simple way to add a different audio track to your video. It's called AudioSwap, and we're trying it out on Test Tube (http://youtube.com/testtube).

If you'd like to try it on one of your videos, you should first make sure it's alright to have your audio *permanently replaced* for that video. If you're okay with that, head to our AudioSwap page (http://youtube.com/audioswap_main), and click the "Try AudioSwap" button. You'll then be able to access a page showing your video on the right and the audio tracks you can choose from on the left.

Select a genre, artist, and track – don't worry, you can play around with as many as you want before adding one to your video. Keep the length of your video in mind, making sure the audio track you select is as long or longer than your video so your entire video has sound. Once you've selected a track, click the "Publish Video" button. When you're asked if you want to change your audio track, click the "OK" button. Depending on the length of your video, it may take some time to update the audio.

Uploading Videos to YouTube

GENERAL UPLOADING QUESTIONS

Why isn't my video showing up in search?

Depending on site traffic, changes to video information can take 8 hours or more to show up in the search index after they have been uploaded, changed, or removed. This includes changes to tags, ratings, views, and comments. Under extreme site traffic we have seen some videos take over 24 hours to index. To bypass this time you may want to send your friends the link of the video via email or private message.

Note that unless the user name of the uploader is specified as a tag it may not be indexed for a video search. To find a user (and their videos) perform a search for their user name select "Channels" on the left side of the search results.

How long will my video take to upload?

Depending on your connection speed and the size of the video, it can take anywhere from a few minutes to several hours to upload a video. Generally, if you have a high-speed Internet connection you can expect the upload to take somewhere between 1-5 minutes for every 1MB. However, the experience is different for every user because of the variation in connection speeds.

How do I upload a video?

Once you've finished editing your video, made sure it's less than 10 minutes, smaller than 100MB, and in an acceptable format, you're ready to upload it.

1. Click "Upload Videos" in the upper-right-hand corner of any YouTube page.
2. Enter as much information about your video as possible, including Title, Description, Tags, and Category. The more information you include, the easier it is for users to find your video!
3. Click the "Go upload a file" button.
4. In the next window, click the "Browse" button to browse for the video file. Select the file you want to upload.
5. Determine if you want your video set to Public or Private.
6. Click the "Upload Video" button.

How long are my videos available on YouTube?

> Videos stay on YouTube until the members who uploaded them choose to take them down. Videos which violate the Terms of Use (http://www.youtube.com/t/terms) may be taken down by YouTube.

Do I have to sign up to upload videos?

Yes. Since videos are attached to your profile, you must sign up as a member to upload videos. Becoming a member also allows you to save videos, create Playlists, and leave comments, among many other features.

Can I replace a video and retain the old view count, comments, and ratings?

There is currently no way to replace an old video with a new one and retain the original view count, comments or ratings. You'll have to start over with your newer video.

Also, our system runs a checksum on all video files that are uploaded to avoid duplicate videos. Simply changing the file name will not resolve this. Please remove the video and edit its length or compression. Then you should be able to upload the video again.

VIDEO FORMATS

What video file formats can I upload?

YouTube accepts video files from most digital cameras, camcorders, and cell phones in the .WMV, .AVI, .MOV, and .MPG file formats.

What's the best format to upload for high quality?

We recommend the following settings:

- MPEG4 (Divx, Xvid) format
- 320x240 resolution
- MP3 audio
- 30 frames per second

Resizing your video to these specifications before uploading will help your videos look better on YouTube.

File Size and Length Limits

How long/large can my video be?

All videos uploaded to YouTube have a 100MB file size limit. The longer the video is, the more compression will be required to fit it into that size. For that reason, most videos on YouTube are under five minutes long and there is a 10-minute length limit for all videos.

Is there a limit to how many videos I can upload?

We don't have any limit for the number of videos you can upload, and don't foresee adding a ceiling anytime in the future. So start making videos and upload as many as you'd like—it's more content for the whole YouTube community to enjoy!

SOLVING UPLOAD ISSUES

My upload's been running a long time and hasn't completed. What should I do?

Uploading a video can take several hours, depending on the length of your video and the demand on the servers. If your video upload is taking longer than 24 hours to complete, we recommend canceling the upload, checking the length and settings for your video, and uploading it again.

What does "Invalid file format error" mean?

"Invalid file format error" means that your video is in a format that our system doesn't accept. We accept most file formats, including .wmv, .mov, .mpg, or .avi. If your video meets these minimum requirements and still won't upload, it may be due to a problem with the video compression you are using. We recommend the MPEG4 (Divx, Xvid) format at 320x240 resolution with MP3 audio.

If you're using Windows Movie Maker, it's also possible that you tried to upload your .MSWMM file. This is not an actual movie file. An .MSWMM file is a Windows Movie Maker project file. If you're satisfied with your movie, choose the "Save Movie File" option under the "File" menu to create a movie file that can be uploaded to YouTube.

AFTER UPLOADING YOUR VIDEO

Editing Video Information

How do I change the default thumbnail for my video?

While we may add this feature in the future, there is currently no way to change the screen shot that we capture from your videos for thumbnails.

What you could do in the meantime is edit the video so it is just a little bit shorter and then upload this new edited video to the site. YouTube will grab a different screen shot of the new video because the length of the video is then different.

YouTube

How do I remove one of my videos?

To remove one of your videos, simply log in, click the "My Videos" link in the upper right corner of the homepage and click the "Remove Video" button below the video you'd like to remove. You can only remove videos that you have uploaded yourself.

How do I change or add to the information I entered about my video?

1. Click the "My Videos" link in the upper right corner.
2. Click the "Edit Video Information" link under the video you want to edit.
3. From the next screen, you can change, add to, or delete whatever information you'd like about your video, including permissions settings (allowing comments, responses, ratings, etc.).

PROMOTING YOUR VIDEOS

Why isn't my video showing up in search?

Depending on site traffic, changes to video information can take 8 hours or more to show up in the search index after they have been uploaded, changed, or removed. This includes changes to tags, ratings, views, and comments. Under extreme site traffic we have seen some videos take over 24 hours to index. To bypass this time you may want to send your friends the link of the video via email or private message.

Note that unless the user name of the uploader is specified as a tag it may not be indexed for a video search. To find a user (and their videos) perform a search for their user name select "Channels" on the left side of the search results.

What are tags? How do I add them?

Tags are keywords that describe videos. For example, a surfing video might be tagged with "surfing," "water," and "waves." Users who enjoy watching surfing videos can then search for any of those terms and that video will show up in their search results. Tags help you label videos you upload so that other people can find them more easily.

Add tags to your videos by clicking the "My Videos" link and selecting "Edit Video Info." Enter as many tags as you'd like into the Tags field and click the "Update Video Info" button at the bottom of the page.

How do I tell my friends I have a new video?

YouTube lets you notify all your friends and admirers when you've posted a new video masterpiece. Here are three ways to let them know:

1. Share your video or your entire Playlist.
2. Have them subscribe to your Channel.
3. Post the video to your blog.

What should I put in my video description?

To best promote your video, you'll want its description to be both accurate and interesting. Here are a few tips to help you get started:

Make your description clear and specific

Your video should stand out from the crowd. Try to determine what content it contains that will help users find it and distinguish it from other videos. Using descriptive language in complete sentences is a good idea.

Give credit when appropriate.

If people don't know the exact title or other keywords associated with your video, they might search the name of a participant or another website where it's featured. Be sure to include as much information as you feel comfortable, but be careful not to include anything that shouldn't be publicly displayed.

Categorize correctly.

The category into which you place your video is part of its description as well. People are more likely to rate your video highly and watch it more frequently if it's placed in a relevant category.

SOLVING VIDEO STATUS ISSUES

Failed (invalid file format)

This status message means that the file type of your video isn't supported by our site. YouTube does not currently accept videos in Flash (.flv) format. You may need to try using software other than the software that came with your camera, such as Windows Movie Maker (included with every Windows installation), or Apple iMovie. By opening your video file with one of these programs and then saving as .avi, .mpg, .wmv, or .mov, you should be able to upload your video with no problems.

Rejected (Terms of Use violation)

The video may have been rejected due to a Terms of Use or copyright violation. Please review our Terms of Use (http://www.youtube.com/t/terms) and Copyright FAQ (http://www.youtube.com/t/dmca_policy).

Failed (unable to convert video file)

This message means that your video is in a format that our converters don't recognize. Try converting the video into a different format with a converter or editing program and then uploading it again.

Rejected (duplicate upload)

This message means that the video you have uploaded already exists within our system. We run a checksum on all video files that are uploaded to avoid duplicate videos. Simply changing the file name will not resolve this. Please try editing the video again. Changing the video length or compression should allow the video to upload.

Failed (empty .mov file)

This error message is only related to QuickTime movies. It occurs when a movie is saved from the QuickTime Player and the "Save as a reference movie" radio button is selected. This creates a small .mov file that points to the full-length video on the hard drive. When you upload this smaller .mov, it doesn't contain actual video content, and can;t be converted by our system.

To ensure that your video converts properly, make sure to select the "Save as a self-contained movie" radio button before saving your video from QuickTime.

THE YOUTUBE COMMUNITY

Interacting with Videos

Rating Videos

What does the video rating represent?

A video's rating represents the average of all ratings it has been given by users since it was uploaded.

I'm unable to rate videos. How do I fix this?

You'll need to be logged in to your account and have a confirmed email address to rate videos.

If you're logged in and aren't able to rate, your email address may not be confirmed. To request a confirmation email, log in and click

Video Comments the "Upload" button in the upper right corner of any YouTube page. Enter your email and click the "Send Confirmation" button. If you still don't see it in your Inbox, try looking in your spam folder.

If you've clicked the link in the confirmation email and are still having trouble, try deleting your browser's cache and cookies, relaunching your browser, and logging back in to YouTube.

I commented on a video, but my comment isn't appearing. What happened?

There is a slight delay for comments to appear on a video once they're posted. Usually, a comment will appear in a few minutes if you refresh the page.

It's also possible that the owner of the video has required approval for all comments on the video. In that case, your comment won't appear until the owner approves it.

I am unable to comment on videos. How do I fix this?

Your email address may not be confirmed. To request a confirmation email: go to the "Upload" button at the top of our website after logging in. You might want to try looking in your spam folder if you can't see it in your Inbox. If you have confirmed by clicking the link in the email you received and are still having trouble you might want to try deleting your browser's cache and cookies, relaunch your browser, and log in to YouTube again.

YouTube

Clearing browser cache

To find out how to clear your cache, click your browser:

- Internet Explorer 7
- Internet Explorer 6
- Firefox 2.x
- Firefox 1.x
- Safari

Internet Explorer 7

1. Click "Start" and select "Control Panel".
(Note: With Windows XP Classic View click the Windows "Start" button and select "Settings" and "Control Panel").
2. Open the "Internet Options" icon.
3. Click the "General" tab if it isn't selected already.
4. Click the "Delete" button.
5. Under the heading "Temporary Internet files," click "Delete Files".
6. Click "OK" to exit.

Internet Explorer 6

1. Click "Start" and select "Control Panel".
(Note: With Windows XP Classic View click the Windows "Start" button and select "Settings" and "Control Panel").
2. Open the "Internet Options" icon.
3. Click the "General" tab if it isn't selected already.
4. Under the heading "Temporary Internet files," click "Delete Files...".
5. Click "OK" to exit.

Mozilla Firefox 2

1. Open Mozilla Firefox and click on the "Tools" menu.
2. Select "Options" then "Advanced". (top right)
3. Click the "Network" tab.
4. Under the "Cache" heading, click the "Clear Now" button.
5. Click "OK" to exit.

Mozilla Firefox 1.x

1. Open Mozilla Firefox on the "Tools" menu.
2. Select "Options" then the "Privacy" icon.
3. Click "Clear" across from the Cache option.
4. Click "OK" to exit.

Safari

1. From the Safari menu, click "Empty Cache".
2. When asked "Are you sure you want to empty the cache?", click "Empty".
3. Click "Done".
4. Reload the page.

Clearing browser cookies

To find out how to clear cookies, click your browser:

- Internet Explorer 7
- Internet Explorer 6
- Firefox 2.x
- Firefox 1.x
- Safari

YouTube

(**Please note:** while clearing your cookies may resolve the problem, it will also remove your saved settings for sites you've previously visited.)

Internet Explorer 7

1. Click "Start" and select "Control Panel".
(Note: With Windows XP Classic View click the Windows "Start" button and select "Settings" and "Control Panel").
2. Open the Internet Options icon.
3. Click the "General" tab if it isn't selected already.
4. Under the Browsing history section, click the "Delete" button.
5. Click the "Delete cookies" button.
6. Select "Yes" if a box appears to confirm.
7. Click "OK" to close the window.

Internet Explorer 6

1. Click "Start" and select "Control Panel". (Note: Windows XP Classic View click the Windows "Start" button and select "Settings" and "Control Panel").
2. Open the "Internet Options" icon.
3. Click the "General" tab if it isn't selected already.
4. Under the heading "Temporary Internet files," click on "Delete Cookies...".
5. Click "OK" for the "Delete all cookies in the Temporary Internet Files folder?" prompt.
6. Click "OK" to exit.

Mozilla Firefox 2.x

1. In Mozilla Firefox select "Tools" from the file menu.
2. Select "Options".
3. Under the "Private Data" heading, click the "Clear Now button".
4. Click "OK" to exit.

Mozilla Firefox 1.x

1. In Mozilla Firefox select "Tools" from the file menu.
2. Select "Options".
3. Click the "Privacy" icon in the top panel.
4. Click the "Cookies" tab.
5. Check the "Clear Cookies Now" button.
6. Click "OK" to save and close.

Safari

1. Go to the "Safari" drop down menu.
2. Select "Preferences".
3. Select the "Security" icon at the top panel.
4. From the Security dialog box, click "Bookmarks".
5. Click "Show Cookies".
6. From the Cookie dialog box, click to choose cookies from youtube.com, and click "Remove" alternatively, if you want to delete all cookies, click "Remove All".
7. Click "Done".

How do I edit or delete a comment I made on someone else's video?

You can't edit or delete comments you make on other people's videos. Once you've made a comment, it can only be removed or moderated by the video owner.

How do I remove a comment from one of my videos?

1. Watch the video with the comment you would like to remove.
2. Scroll down to the "Comments & Responses" section and locate the comment that you would like to remove.
3. Click the "Remove" link beneath the comment.

You can also change how comments are posted to each of your videos. If you edit the properties for a video, you have the option to allow all comments, require approval for each comment, or block all comments.

How do I comment on a video I'm watching?

To post a text comment for a video, start typing in the "Comment on this video" field or click the "Post a text comment" link below the video player. Then, enter your comment and click the "Post Comment" button. Remember to keep your comments respectful and relevant, so they can be enjoyed by the full YouTube community!

How do I control commenting on my videos?

1. Login to your YouTube account.
2. Go to the "My Videos" page (http://www.youtube.com/my_videos).
3. Click the "Edit Video Info" button under the video you wish to edit.
4. Under "Sharing," you will find the "Allow Comments" options.

- To require your approval for each comment, choose "Yes, with Approval."
- To allow comments without approval, select "Yes, Automatic."
- To turn comments off, select "No."
5. Make sure you click the "Update Video Info" button when you are done.

Video Responses

How do I make/upload a video response?

To respond to a video, click the "Post a Video Response" link below the video player. You will then be given three options for choosing your response video: Record a Video, Choose a Video, and Upload a Video.

Record a Video

YouTube will automatically attempt to detect your computer's settings if you choose to respond via QuickCapture. Click the "Allow" button in the window that pops up so that YouTube can access your camera and microphone. Before you can begin recording your webcam response, be sure to enter information into all the fields on the left hand side of the screen.

Choose a Video

The dropdown here allows you to respond with any video you've already posted. One thing to keep in mind—your video can only be used as a response once. If you've used a video as a response in the past and want to use it for a new response, it will no longer be listed as the earlier response.

Upload a Video

This works pretty similarly to the normal upload process. Click the "Upload a Video" link. Enter all of your video's information, then click either "Go upload a file" to upload a file, or "Use QuickCapture" if you decide to use your webcam after all.

Why isn't my video response appearing?

If you don't see a video response you have posted, it may be because the owner of the original video has to approve your response before it will appear. Once the owner approves your video, it will appear as a video response under the original.

How do I control video responses to my videos?

1. Login to your YouTube account.
2. Go to the "My Videos" page (http://www.youtube.com/my_videos).
3. Click the "Edit Video Info" button under the video you wish to edit.
4. Under "Sharing," you will find the "Allow Video Responses" options.
   - To require your approval for each video response, choose "Yes, with Approval."
   - To allow video responses without approval, select "Yes, Automatic."
   - To turn video responses off, select "No."
5. Make sure you click the "Update Video Info" button when you are done.

YouTube

6. **How do I approve/deny a video response to my video?**

7. If someone responds to your video, you'll get an email with their username and the title of the responding video. Click the "go to the Video Responses section of your Inbox" link in that email or just click "Inbox" in the upper right corner of the homepage. You'll be taken to a screen showing you several representative thumbnails and other information about the video. From your Inbox, you can approve, reject, or take no action on any pending video responses by selecting that action from the drop-down menu at the bottom.

YouTube

INTERACTING WITH OTHER USERS

Messages and Friend Invites

How do I add a Friend to my Contact List?

Once you've added your friends to one of your contact lists, you can easily share your favorite videos with lots of people at once. Here's how to add a friend to your list:

1. Log in.
2. Go to your friend's profile page: http://www.youtube.com/profile?user=USERNAME
3. Within his or her "Connect with USERNAME" section, click the "Add as friend" button.
4. Choose one of your contact lists from the drop-down menu.
5. Click the "Send Invite" button.

How do I send a private message to another user?

You can use YouTube to send private messages and comments to your friends. Start by clicking your friend's username next to one of their videos. Once you're on their Channel page, click the "Send Message" link underneath their thumbnail. You can then write a message just like an email and attach a link to any video from your favorites or uploads. When you're done, click "Send Message" and your friend will be able to view it in their YouTube Inbox. They'll also receive an email letting them know they've got a new message to read.

What does it mean to be another user's Friend on YouTube?

Friends, Family, and any other lists you decide to create allow you to quickly share videos with a large group of people. Once you've added someone to your contact list, you can move them to your Friends list or any other list you've made. Then, you can easily send interesting videos to everyone on that list by clicking the "Share Video" link under the video player, checking the box next to the list you want to use, and clicking the "Send" button.

You can also set privacy settings for your contact lists, which allows you to make videos visible only to members of that list. This makes it easy to share personal videos only with friends or family, and other YouTube users will not be able to see them.

How do I find out if someone has sent me a private message?

Every time someone sends you a new private message, you'll get a notification email with a link to the message, unless you have turned these notifications off from your Account page. You can see all the private messages you've received by clicking "General Messages" in your YouTube Inbox, or by clicking the number in parentheses next to your username at the top of the page.

How do I accept a friend invite from another user?

When someone invites you to be their YouTube friend, you'll receive an email telling you how to accept their invitation. Clicking the link in their email will send you to the "Friend Invites" section of your Inbox, once you've logged in. From there, click on the checkbox next to the invite, and you can choose to "Accept Invitations" or "Reject Invitations" in the drop-down menu. Finish by clicking the "Apply to Selected Invites" button.

I'm unable to send or receive private messages. How do I fix this?

Your email address may not be confirmed. Log in and click the "Upload Video" link at the top of the homepage to request a confirmation email. If you still don't see the email, try looking in your spam folder. If you have confirmed by clicking the link in the confirmation email and are still having trouble, you might want to try deleting your browser's <u>cache and cookies</u>, relaunching your browser, and logging back in to YouTube.

How do I invite my friends to join YouTube?

The quickest way to invite your friends to join YouTube is to log in, go to your Account page and click the "Invite More Friends" button under "Friends & Contacts." Invite one friend, or a bunch, by adding commas between their email addresses. Then add whatever personal message you'd like, and don't forget to fill in your name so they know who's inviting them. Click "Send Invite," and then wait for them to join up and start sharing videos with you!

SUBSCRIPTIONS

How do I unsubscribe from someone's videos or favorites?

Once you're tired of being subscribed to someone's videos or favorites, just go into your account and look under "My Subscriptions" or look into that person's profile page and click "Unsubscribe." Simple as that.

How do I subscribe to someone's videos?

1. Go to the member's profile page.
2. To subscribe to that member's videos, click the orange "Subscribe" button or the "Subscribe To Videos" link.

How do I unsubscribe another user from my videos?

1. Log in and go to the My Account page (http://www.youtube.com/my_account).
2. In the "Subscriptions and Subscribers" section, click the "Subscribers to My Videos" link.
3. Click the "Unsubscribe" button for anyone you'd like to remove.

STREAMS

What are Streams?

Streams allow you to create a YouTube room to interact with other users while sharing videos. Everyone who's part of each room can chat with each other in real time as the videos play and add videos from their Favorites, QuickList, or by pasting in links. Streams have two basic areas: the video (on the left) and the chat (on the right).

Videos

Along the top of the stream, you'll see thumbnails and partial titles for all of the videos currently in the room; clicking one will move it to the player for you to watch.

Chatting

On the right side of the screen, you'll see a list of all the YouTube users in the room, the ongoing chat, and an open text box where you can type your comments. Just type in the box and click "Enter" to see your comment appear. It will appear in the conversation with your currently watched video as the icon (unless you uncheck the "Include current video" checkbox).

How do I join a Stream?

There are two ways to find a stream you want to join: follow the link from an email or IM, or browse through the currently active streams (http://www.youtube.com/streams_main). If you're not already logged in to YouTube, you'll need to log in on the way there.

After you pick the stream you want to join, you'll see a welcome message from the Stream owner, and you will appear in the chat as a new member of the room. You can only be in one Stream at a time.

How do I manage users in a Stream?

If another user in the room is being obnoxious or inappropriate, you can flag them to the owner of the room by hovering over their username and clicking "Inappropriate." Only the owner of the room can actually kick out or ban users from the room, however.

If you're the stream owner, you can click "Admin Users" in the lower right corner of the screen. You'll then see a list of current users in your stream, along with their user status and the last video they watched. You'll also be able to take disciplinary actions against specific users. Under the "Action" column, you can select "Kick – for 30 seconds," to kick a user out of your stream temporarily, or "Ban from stream," to remove them permanently.

Why/how did I get kicked out of a Stream?

The owner of the stream has the power to kick users out of the stream temporarily or ban them permanently. Owners can also give other users Administrator rights to help with managing the room. The owner or administrators may have thought the videos or comments you were posting were inappropriate. Normal users can also flag you as an inappropriate user, in which case the owner receives a notification email.

How do I add videos to a Stream?

If the owner has allowed everyone to add videos to the stream (or if you're included in the approved group), there are three easy ways you can add more.

Load Watched Videos or Load Quicklist

Clicking these buttons will load your recently watched videos or Quicklist. The first video on the list will automatically load into the player and will be shared with the rest of the room when you start to watch. Clicking the first button on a video in this list preloads it; the second button shares it with the room and opens it in the player; and the third button deletes it from the list.

Add Video by URL

You can also add a video by pasting the full URL from the main YouTube site into the Video URL box at the bottom and clicking the "Add Video by URL" button.

How do I create a Stream?

You can create your own stream from the TestTube page (www.youtube.com/testtube), or just go directly to the creation page. The only required field is the title, and the rest are self-explanatory. Once you click "Save Stream Info," your room will be created and you'll enter it as the first member.

CHANNELS

General Channel Questions

How do I customize my Channel?

Three links under Channel Settings on your account page will help you show your personality through your channel.

Edit Channel Info

This is where you can edit all your channel's basic settings and the information about yourself that you choose to make public.

A lot of people like to give their channel a title and description to help clarify what they're really interested in. You have two options to create a profile picture: you can display the last video you uploaded or select a more permanent picture from "My Videos." You can also choose whether you'd like to display comments and bulletins on your Channel.

Feel free to fill in whatever personal information you're comfortable with in the provided fields—none of them are mandatory.

Customize Channel Theme

This is where you get to show off your artistic talent. You can choose to use one of our basic color themes, create your own color schemes for everything from the background to the fonts, or even link to a URL that has an image you'd like to display as your background.

How do I get a personal thumbnail?

Your thumbnail, or profile icon, is a still frame from one of your videos. From your Edit Channel Info page, you have the choice to set your thumbnail to come from your most recently uploaded video or from one selected video. If you have a thumbnail image in mind that doesn't appear in any of your videos, one alternative is to create a short (5 seconds or so) video of the scene of your choice. Once you've uploaded it, set your profile icon to come from that video within "My Videos."

How do I change my age in my account?

There's currently no way to change your age in your account.
You do have the option to hide your age, if you'd like to do so.

What is a Channel/Profile?

Everyone who has joined YouTube can view their personal information on their Channel or Profile page. It's a centralized location where other users can see your public videos, favorites, bulletins, comments, subscribers and video log. Users can also see stats about you, like how long you've been a YouTube member, how old you are, and how many videos you've watched.

Your Channel's also an easy place for people to connect with you, to send you a message, share a channel, add you as a friend, or add comments to your Channel.

How do I hide my age on my Profile page?

If you don't want your age to display on your profile page, you can follow these steps to remove it:

1. Log in and go to the My Account page.

2. Under Channel Settings, click the "Personal Info" link.

3. On the next page, select the "Do not display your age on your public profile" option.

4. Click the "Update Channel" button.

Profile Comments and Bulletins

How do I send/delete bulletins from my Profile?

To post a bulletin, click the "Broadcast a message" link under Bulletins on your channel. Fill in the subject line and body, and select a video to attach from the drop-down menu if you'd like. Click the "Submit Post" button. Your bulletin post will appear on your channel shortly.

Your bulletins will automatically expire after 30 days. There is no other way to remove them, however, so make sure you only write what you want to see on your channel for the next month!

What are Bulletins?

Bulletins are your opportunity to broadcast messages to your YouTube friends when they visit your Channel or their own. Post new bulletins to show what you've been doing, your thoughts on your newest videos, thoughts on medieval literature, whatever!

How do I delete comments from my Profile?

If you'd like to remove someone's comments from your Profile, click the "See All Comments" link in the Comments box. This will allow you to put a check next to any comments you'd like to remove. Then just click the "Remove Selected" button and they'll disappear.

How do I post comments on another person's Profile?

Once you've reached the other member's profile page, scroll to the bottom left and look into the Comments box. Click the "Add Comment" link. Then enter your comment, choose a video to attach (if you'd like), and click the "Submit Comment" button.

VLOG

What is my Vlog and how do I create it?

Your Vlog, or video weblog, is an easy way for you to post videos from one of your Playlists to your Profile page and insert customized titles and comments to them.

- Go to your Profile page.

- In the Videos section, click the "Playlists" link.

- Click the "Create New Playlist" button. Clicking that button will take you to a page where you can first add some personality to your Playlist, with a title, description, and tags.

- Click the box next to "Use this playlist as my Video Log in my Channel" and the videos from this list will automatically appear on your profile page.

- You can add videos to your Vlog by saving to that playlist or transferring videos from other playlists or your Favorites.

There's another way to create your Vlog! Just open any of the Playlists you've already created and click "Set as Vlog."

How do I change the videos in my Vlog?

To add a video to your Vlog, find the video you'd like to add and choose "Save to Favorites" under the video player. From the dropdown menu, select the playlist set as your Vlog and click "OK."

To remove videos from your Vlog, select the playlist set as your Vlog from My Playlists.

YouTube

To delete the videos from all your Playlists, check the box to the left of each video you want to remove and click the "Remove Videos" button. To move them to another Playlist, check the box to the left of each video you want to move. Then select the Playlist where you would like to move the video from the drop-down menu provided.

You can also change the order of the Playlist by changing the numbers to the right of each video and clicking the "Rearrange" button.

How do I edit the descriptions in my Vlog?

Beside every video in your Vlog is an "Edit Post" link. Clicking that link will give you the choice to allow the video to display its original title and description or a new title and description which you enter into the provided fields. Once you've finished making your changes and additions, click "Submit" and they will appear beside that video in your Vlog.

ACCOUNT AND POLICIES

Account Information

Account Types

What's the difference between a regular YouTube account and all of these other accounts (Director, Musician, Comedian)?

All accounts share the basic features on YouTube like uploading, commenting, sharing, video responses, etc. Each of the specialized account types offers different customization options:

Director:
Allows custom items and logo on Profile pages.

Musician:
Allows custom logo, genre and tour date information, and CD purchase links on Profile.

Comedian:
Allows custom logo, style and show date information, and CD purchase links on Profile.

What's new with Director Accounts?

Director Accounts are perfect for people who take their videos seriously. Whether you own your own production studio or are just passionate about home videos, a Director Account can offer a lot of advantages.

Now you can convert to a Director Account without filling out an application. From your Channel Info page, click on "change channel type" and you can select "Director" as the type of account you'd like. Once you've converted to a Director Account, you'll be able to create or choose your own customized logo.

What is a Guru account?

Guru accounts are for people who are experts in… something! If you're a gourmet chef, successful investor, or creative clothing designer, you might want to look into getting a Guru account. Advantages include being able to create a custom logo, genre, and links to your other websites from your Profile.

There are two ways you can get a Guru account:

Specify the type of account you'd like when you first sign up for a new account.

or

Convert your account from your Channel Info page.

How do I get a Director/Comedian/Musician/Guru account?

There are two ways to get a Director, Comedian, Musician, or Guru account:

1. Specify the type of account you'd like when you first sign up for a new account.
2. Go to the "Channel Info" section (http://www.youtube.com/my_profile) of your account and click on the "change channel type" link.

Closing Accounts

How do I close my account?

Please make sure you have removed your videos before closing your account.

To close your account:

1. Log in with your user name and password.
2. Click the "My Account" link in the upper-right-hand corner.
3. In the "Account Settings" section, click the "Close Account" button.
4. Enter the reason you're closing the account, and your password, then click the "Close My Account" button.
5. Click the "Log Out" link in the upper-right-hand corner.

How do I re-open an account I previously closed?

You can't re-open the account directly. To request that your account be re-opened, please email us by clicking "Contact us" on You-Tube website in "Help Center"

Why was my account suspended?

Your account was suspended due to repeated or severe violation of our Terms of Use (http://www.youtube.com/t/terms). Users with suspended or terminated accounts are prohibited from creating new accounts or accessing YouTube's community features.

YouTube

Username and Password

I forgot my user name or password. How do I log back into the site?

If you forgot your password, you can retrieve it <u>here</u> (http://www.youtube.com/forgot).

If you forgot your user name, you can retrieve it <u>here</u> (http://www.youtube.com/forgot_username).

How do I change my password?

1. Log in with your user name and current password.
2. Click the "My Account" link in the upper-right-hand corner.
3. Under Account Settings, click the "Password & Email" link.
4. Enter your current YouTube password.
5. Enter your new password in the "New Password" field and the "Retype New Password" field.
6. Click the "Update" button.

Can I change my YouTube username?

Currently, you cannot change your username— there is simply too much information tied to each account. You may, however, sign up for a new account with the username that you desire.

How do I change the email address tied to my YouTube user name?

1. Log in with your user name and password.
2. Click the "My Account" link in the upper-right-hand corner.
3. Under Account Settings, click the "Email Options" link.
4. Click the "change address" link.
5. Type your new email address into the Email Address field.
6. Click the "Send Email" button.
7. Check to see if you've received an email from YouTube in the account you entered. (If you don't see it after several minutes, check your Spam folder to see if it was filtered out of your main Inbox.)
8. Once you've opened the email, click the included link. You will be brought to a page that says, "Your email has been confirmed."

I tried to recover my user name, but the email I received was blank. What does this mean?

If you receive an email without a user name, it's because we have no accounts associated with your email address. It's possible that your account registration didn't complete properly or that you signed up with a different email address.

If you think you signed up with an alternate email address, then you may want to enter that email address into our "Forgot Username" form (http://www.youtube.com/forgot_username). If that doesn't help, try signing up again (http://www.youtube.com/signup).

NOTE: ALWAYS REFER TO WWW.YOUTUBE.COM FOR THEIR CURRENT POLICES AND NEWS.

YouTube

NOTES

YouTube

YouTube

YouTube

Printed in the United States
137341LV00002B/3/A